I, FRANCIS

I, FRANCIS

40th Anniversary Edition

CARLO CARRETTO

---

*Translated from the Italian
by Robert R. Barr*

Foreword by Jon M. Sweeney

ORBIS BOOKS
Maryknoll, New York 10545

Founded in 1970, Orbis Books endeavors to publish works that enlighten the mind, nourish the spirit, and challenge the conscience. The publishing arm of the Maryknoll Fathers and Brothers, Orbis seeks to explore the global dimensions of the Christian faith and mission, to invite dialogue with diverse cultures and religious traditions, and to serve the cause of reconciliation and peace. The books published reflect the views of their authors and do not represent the official position of the Maryknoll Society. To learn more about Maryknoll and Orbis Books, please visit our website at www.orbisbooks.com.

Library of Congress Cataloging-in-Publication Data

Names: Carretto, Carlo, author. | Barr, Robert R., translator.
Title: I, Francis / Carlo Carretto ; translated from the Italian by Robert R. Barr.
Other titles: Io Francesco. English
Description: 40th anniversary edition. | Maryknoll, New York : Orbis Books, [2022] | Translation of: Io Francesco. | Summary: "The 40th anniversary edition of an Orbis classic-Francis of Assisi's spirituality and life explained in the inimitable voice of Carlo Carretto"—Provided by publisher.
Identifiers: LCCN 2022003124 (print) | LCCN 2022003125 (ebook) | ISBN 9781626984783 (trade paperback) | ISBN 9781608339402 (epub)
Subjects: LCSH: Francis, of Assisi, Saint, 1182-1226.
Classification: LCC BX4700.F6 C327513 2022 (print) | LCC BX4700.F6 (ebook) | DDC 271/.302—dc23/eng/20220215
LC record available at https://lccn.loc.gov/2022003124
LC ebook record available at https://lccn.loc.gov/2022003125

Contents

Foreword
to the Fortieth
Anniversary Edition

As the title indicates, this is not a book about Francis of Assisi, but one that recreates his heart. How could Carlo Carretto presume to do such a thing?

The German edition, published in 1984, reflected its publisher's discomfort with the notion, when Herder published *I, Francis* as *Was Franzikus uns heute sagt*, "What Francis is telling us today." But that's not quite right. After the short preface penned in Carretto's voice, it is Francis of Assisi who is speaking.

I, Francis is, in effect, a found writing of the great saint, who left so little autobiographical writings behind. And Carretto's Francis strikes me as accurate to the historical saint: playful, dramatic, selfless, yet with a healthy ego, and critical of a world that forgets its Creator, and a Church that likes to forget the world. *I, Francis* reveals the world's most popular saint fighting the worldliness of his Church, which seems focused more often on greed, power, and authority than on the generosity and love of the Gospel taught and lived by Jesus. But how did Carretto come to grasp Francis so well?

"God's call is mysterious; it comes in the darkness of faith," Carretto wrote in an earlier book, *Letters from the Desert*, prefacing some of his own autobiographical remarks. We might easily agree with the first statement, but the second is more difficult, unless you too are a contemplative. Carlo was a contemplative activist, which is even more misunderstood than a contemplative writer. His actions and opinions, both bold and strong, had roots in a prayer practice of careful listening. He did not claim always to know why or what he was doing with his life, beyond responding to God's desires.

There are three big movements to note in the Carretto biography—times when the call of God left "a permanent mark," as Carlo explained it. First was his conversion at 18. Already a schoolteacher by then, Carlo attended the annual Lenten parish mission in town and was bored by the sermons, but convicted of his need for salvation by the eyes of the missioner.

Second, was at 23, when Carlo was about to marry. This time, his description reminds me of the impetuously faithful Francis of Assisi: "I was praying in an empty church where I had gone to escape from my state of inner confusion. I heard the same voice that I had heard during my confession with the old missionary: 'Marriage is not for you. You will offer your life to me. I shall be your Lover forever.'" This is how Francis also began hearing God's voice, when he was alone praying in the empty and dilapidated church of San Damiano, when he heard God say, "Go and rebuild my church."

Third, for Carlo, was at 44, when he heard a call—"I experienced it deeply in the depth which only faith can provide and where darkness is absolute," he explains—to the desert of North Africa. Carlo was at that time the influential lay leader of a large international youth movement called Catholic Action. For most of us, such a call—in darkness—might leave us wanting to wait a little while longer for the morning light. But Carlo resigned his position, and left for Africa.

Which brings me to the other saint essential for grasping Carlo's love for Saint Francis; Carlo really found Francis through Saint Charles de Foucauld (1858–1916). Briefly, after visits to the Holy Land in the 1880s, Charles began discerning his own call to religious life with various religious orders, until finally, ordained a priest in 1901, he felt inspired to leave for the Saharan desert of Algeria in order to live in imitation of aspects of Christ rarely recognized, "with an unquenchable love for the hidden life, and for obedience, the state of voluntary humility," as biographer René Bazin puts it. Years later, on December 1, 1916, Charles was murdered there by a local gang who despised his colonialism, and maybe his faith, despite the humility and hiddenness of his life. Foucauld's was a pioneering but quiet work, without converts or even noticeable effect. "God had only made him for sowing," says Bazin.

Carlo followed in these footsteps, without any desire for martyrdom, just wanting to be one of who by then were called the Little Brothers of Jesus, a religious congregation formed in 1933 in Foucauld's name. Carlo left behind everything and everyone he knew to enter that desert to pray and be a silent witness to the presence of the hidden Christ. Francis of Assisi did similarly 725 years earlier. And as Carlo says in the preface here, Francis's is the story of how we can "find within us the power of believing in the possibility of renewing the world."

Carlo did not die in the North African desert, as Charles de Foucauld had almost gladly done. Quite the contrary. Carlo remained in the desert for twenty years, but did not die until 1988—on the Feast of Saint Francis—twenty-four years after leaving the Sahara to return to Italy. He wrote *I, Francis* after those twenty years in north Africa, after returning to the troubles of the world and the Church.

What does the desert have to do with the rest of us, wherever we live? Simply this: Only a counter-cultural faith will change the world.

I believe that each time we rediscover the teachings and life of Francis of Assisi, we begin to see the Gospel again. This is St. Francis's evergreen gift—revealing time and again the importance of being reborn, of listening for the Holy Spirit, of creatively responding to divine inspiration, of seeing Christ in the faces of his creatures. This is absolutely true to the way and teachings of Jesus, and yet mostly untried by Christians ever since. And this is what Carretto accomplishes in this classic.

We meet the God who is poor. In fact, at the moment when St. Francis realizes the meaning of Christ's incarnation, Carlo has him enthusing: "All sadness would have to be banished. Every one of us was lord of the world. Every pauper was rich. Every heart was satiated." In those lines we hear clearly the Beatitudes, which Francis embodied fully, followed immediately by this, revealing not only St. Francis's vision but the charism of Pope Francis: "Every project was possible."

I also like how Carretto fixes the long-held hagiographical assumption of St. Francis's naivete, which assumes that the convert who heard God saying "Go and rebuild my church" took it only literally and started gathering stones. The autobiographical musings of I, Francis have the saint explaining:

> At once I had set about attempting to repair the crumbling walls of Saint Damian. But I quickly realized that the Lord's words must have meant something much more vast. They must have had to do with the Church of Rome.

God help us, still.

Renewal of the Church always tracks with St. Francis, as it did 800 years ago when the spiritual movement he founded rapidly became the fastest-growing religious order the world had ever seen; as it did when Christians discovered Francis in the years after the destruction and in the hopelessness of post-First World War Europe; as it did when bishops were referring to the witness of Francis of Assisi at the Second Vatican Council sixty years ago; as happened throughout the world in the twentieth century as Francis became the world's most popular saint, well beyond the boundaries of the Roman Church, including among agnostics, atheists, and people of other religious traditions who sense an authentic imprint of the Spirit; and as has been happening in our day when, starting a decade ago, a Jesuit Roman pontiff shocked the world by taking his name from the little poor man from Assisi and then wrote the most important encyclical in a century, *Laudato Si'*. It is from beginning to end a commentary on St. Francis's teachings from eight centuries ago, and it remains to be seen, once again, if counter-cultural faith will save us.

—Jon M. Sweeney

Sources

See *Letters from the Desert*, trans. Rose Mary Hancock (Maryknoll, NY: Orbis Books, 1972), or *Carlo Carretto: Essential Writings*, ed. Robert Ellsberg (Maryknoll, NY: Orbis Books, 2007), 29–32.

René Bazin, *Charles de Foucauld: Hermit and Explorer*, trans. Peter Keelan (London: Burns Oates & Washbourne, 1931), 74, 339.

I, Francis, xv, 18, 62.

Preface
Sainthood—Just a Dream?

At least once in our lives we have dreamed of becoming saints, of being saints.

Stumbling under the weight of the contradictions of our lives, for a fleeting moment we glimpsed the possibility of building within ourselves a place of simplicity and light.

Horrified at our own selfishness, we burst asunder the chains of the senses, at least in our desire, and glimpsed the possibility of true freedom and authentic love.

Bored by a middle-class, conformist life, we suddenly saw ourselves out on the streets of the world—bearers of a message of light and love, love of all sisters and brothers, and ready to offer, on the altar of unconditional love, the witness of a life in which the primacy of poverty and love would make communicating and relating an easy matter.

This is when Francis entered our lives in some way.

It would not be easy to find a Christian—Catholic, Protestant, or Orthodox—who has never identified the notion of human holiness with the figure of Francis of Assisi, and who has not in some measure desired to imitate him.

As Jesus is the basis and ground of everything, as Mary

is the mother par excellence, as Paul is the Apostle of the Gentiles—so Francis, in all Churches, is the incarnation, the ideal figure, of the human being who sets out on the adventure of sainthood and expresses it in a way that is truly universal. Anyone who has ever considered holiness possible in a human being has seen it in the poverty and tenderness of Francis, has joined himself or herself to the prayer of the Canticle of Creatures, has dreamed of going beyond the limits imposed on us by unbelief, the limits of fear, beyond which one should indeed be able to tame wolves and speak to the fishes and the swallows.

I think Francis of Assisi is in the depths of every human being, for all are touched by grace—just as the call to holiness is in the depths of every human being.

And yet at any moment in history, Francis, while profoundly incarnate in history, can be placed outside history as well.

He can be placed with the first Christians, who, as itinerants in the streets of the Roman Empire, bore with them the joy of a message that was really new. He can be placed among the medieval reformers, as the rebuilder of a Church enfeebled by political struggle and threatened by false compromise. He can be placed in the baroque era, challenging, with his strange poverty and humility, the pride of the clerical class, whose priesthood was that of lords of the people instead of as their servants. He can be placed in the world of today as the prototype of the modern man or woman, sallying forth from anguish and isolation to renew the discourse with nature, with human beings, and with God.

Especially with God.

Let me explain what I mean.

If it is true, and it is, that we are living in the most atheistic epoch of all times, it is just as true that it takes practically nothing to reverse the situation.

In the saturated sea of tensions that surrounds us, a sea

prepared and purified by our suffering and earnest searching, it takes only a minimal catalytic factor to provoke a sudden and total precipitation. I have become accustomed to seeing more conversions among the "far" than among the "near"; and when I am invited to talk of God, those most interested are the ones who have always denied God.

So often a "no to everything," thickened to curdling by the spirit of free and genuine thinking and searching, explodes in a "yes to everything" in the presence of the sudden radiation of the Absolute.

Even matter, heretofore seen as empty of God, who would be useless in any event, suddenly lights up, with this Presence that was always present and now returns to speak to us of its deepest mysteries.

Contemporary atheism, in its immense efforts to liberate itself from a bygone religious culture, is on the eve of a radical explosion of faith. Naked, and more transparent, this faith will have acquired a more vital capability of contemplating the oneness of the All as a sign of God's Immanence in things, together with the perfect Transcendence of the triple divine person.

But how shall we begin?

How can we find within us the power of believing in the possibility of renewing the world, of finding peace once more and our lost joy—of feeling hope again, of building upon a rock?

We all have a feeling of having arrived at a critical juncture in history, after a long period of a thousand disasters that has come at last to its final agony.

There are those who speak of an imminent apocalypse, of an atomic terror. We may not wish to go that far, relying on our basic hope. But this is a sorrowful hope, that peace may win out over fear, that fear itself may deter human beings from pushing the nuclear button. We feel ill at ease, lined up as we are behind rows upon rows of machines, and dismayed to discover that technology has led us into a dark, unpleasant tunnel where we can scarcely breathe.

And what are we to say when one gray autumn morning we perceive, coming out of the mist, the little stream where we used to gaily splash and play as children, converted now into a filthy current of water covered with foam and invaded by mountains of garbage—antithetical symbol of a prosperous civilization?

The malaise of which we are conscious at that moment is deep, deeper than we first suspect, and it does us more harm than we think.

In the long term it destroys joy, it takes away our peace. It makes us nervous, and it makes us wicked.

We end up by hating everyone and everything.

And we do not like to think about it, so we toss off some alcohol, or light up a cigarette.

But underneath, it still hurts. And it blocks off the horizons of life.

If we happen to be passing by the school we attended once upon a time, or the place where we used to work, or even the house where we lived in years gone by, perhaps built by our own hands, with our own sweat and effort, and they have gone to rack and ruin, so much that we would hate even to have to go into them again, then even daily toil takes on the hue of something we do in vain.

Not even the steeples of our churches any longer have the power to speak to us, or inspire us.

The only thing that holds any power of attraction for us now is flight, or the desire to taste some new pleasure, even a dangerous one, and we become available for every sort of forbidden adventure.

Even the good fall short. Mothers spend their days away

from their children, fathers are continually having something to do far from home. We have started down the slippery slope, and the boredom we can no longer escape results in dejection, mistrust of society or of our own work, dryness of heart, and the cloying of physical pleasures as a surrogate for values now compromised or destroyed.

A glance at a list of the films "now playing," a walk by night through a railroad terminal where the waiting room has become a public dormitory for uprooted men and women, a few hours spent in an inner-city dispensary where addicts gather in droves for their methadone, are all we need to convince ourselves that we have come to an historical juncture of exceptional critical gravity, and this to an extent never before experienced.

Like an epidemic that has reached the term of its incubation, evil has invaded the whole body of humankind. It is above, it is below, it is within and without, it is everywhere.

A few days ago I revisited the Berlin Wall—that absurdity that lasts and lasts while life goes on around it as if nothing were the matter.

I realized as never before that that wall is but the outward sign of an infinite number of other walls, the walls that divide up people and things. The real wall is within us, and it divides rich from poor, nation from nation, children from parents, human beings from one another, human beings from God.

We are divided, split apart to the depths of our innards, as the Berlin Wall divides Germans from Germans, as Jerusalem is split between Jews and Arabs, as any man or woman may be all alone in the universe around.

Everything is quiet, for the moment—but all ready to explode.

Yes, I truly believe we could be on the eve of the Apocalypse—unless. . . .

❧

Here I am up in the Cave of Narni to spend a few months in solitude. Once more I have yielded to the temptation of the desert, which has always been the love niche where I can encounter the Absolute that is God, and the place where truth bursts out in blossom. The Franciscan solitude of this lofty grotto rivals the dunes of Beni-Abbes, or the harsh desert of Assekrem. At bottom they all spring from the same root; for when Père de Foucauld sought the African desert he was doing what Francis had done when he sought the silence of the Subasio dungeons, or the rough country of Sasso Spico at La Verna.

What counts is God, and the silence of an environment where God is near.

I sought out this hermitage because it is one of the special places of the Franciscan world, where the Saint sojourned on repeated occasions, and where all blends together in a perfect oneness. Forests, bare rock, the architecture, poverty, humility, simplicity, and beauty, all go together to form one of the masterpieces of the Franciscan spirit—an example to the centuries of peace, prayer, silence, ecology, beauty, and the human victory over the contradictions of time.

When we behold these hermitages, abodes of men and women of peace and prayer and joyous acceptance of poverty, we have the answer to the anguished conflicts that torment our civilization.

You see, these rocks say to us, you see, peace is possible. Do not seek for luxury when you build your houses, seek the essentials. Poverty will become beauty then, and liberating harmony—as you can see in this hermitage. Do not destroy forests in order to build factories that swell the ranks of the unemployed and create unrest; help human beings to return to the countryside, to learn again to appreciate a truly well-turned object, to feel the joy of silence and of contact with earth and sky. Do not hoard up money—inflation and greedy people lie in ambush for you; instead, leave the door of your heart open for a dialogue with your brother or sister, for service to the very poor.

Do not prostitute your labor fabricating things that last half a season, consuming what little raw material you have left; but make pails like the one you see here at this well—it has been drawing its water for centuries and is still in use.

The ill you speak of consumerism is a cover. You fill your mouth with words in order to stifle a bad conscience. Even as you speak, you are consumerism's slaves, without any capacity for innovation and imagination.

And then . . .

Unburden yourselves of your fear of your brothers and sisters! Go out to meet them unarmed and meek. They are human beings too, just like you, and they need love and trust, even as you.

Do not be concerned with *"what you are to eat and with what you are to drink"* (Matt. 6:25); be calm, and you shall lack nothing. *"Set your hearts on his kingdom first, and on his righteousness"* (Matt. 6:33), and everything else will be given to you for good measure. *"Each day has enough trouble of its own"* (Matt. 6:34).

Yes, this hermitage speaks. It speaks and says brotherly and sisterly love is possible.

It speaks and says that God is our Father, that creatures are our brothers and sisters, and that peace is joy.

All you have to do is will it.

Try it, brothers and sisters, try it, and you will see that it is possible.

The Gospel is true.

Jesus is the Son of God, and saves humankind.

Nonviolence is more constructive than violence.

Chastity is more pleasurable than impurity.

Poverty is more exciting than wealth.

❧

Try to think about it, sisters and brothers. What an extraordinary adventure lies here before us.

If we put Francis's project into execution we shall be escaping the atomic apocalypse.

Is it not always this way? God proposes peace.

Why not try it?

I, Francis

I was born in Assisi, in Italy, eight hundred years ago. And eight centuries later I still remember a thing or two.

When I ask myself why I have survived so long in people's hearts, Jesus gives me the answer in the Gospel, in the passage called the Beatitudes. The Beatitudes are about earth, but they are still true in heaven. And the answer is, "Blessed are the meek, for they shall possess the land."

Yes, I may as well admit it. I was meek. Or at least I very much wished to be, and not only that, but I tried to do something about it.

If I were still on earth I would still break the same trail. People are tired of violence. They may find it difficult to live in peace with one another, but they very much desire to do so. Instinctively they prefer the lamb to the lion.

I am touched at the thought that anyone yet remembers me, Francis, son of Peter di Bernardone and of. . . . Try to think of the name of my mother. Few know it! But they recall my father's name very well. That is always the way it is. You are still antifeminists! Yet I owe much more to my mother than to my father. She was French, from Provence. She sang very well. And she loved Assisi better than the natives, because she was tasteful.

Now I shall tell you. Pica. That was her name. She was beautiful and sweet, and she had faith.

My father, on the other hand, did not have much faith. He liked money better, and it multiplied in his hands with ease. He was a textile merchant.

Money meant little to me because it had not cost me anything. My father had worked hard to amass his, and ran serious risk of assault and robbery every time one of his caravans went on the road to France and farther. You have to realize that there were robbers in those days too! One had to be very careful, and see them coming. And often enough even that did not suffice.

Yes, money meant little to me. Mine was a different set of values—beauty, song, friendship, glory, and glory especially.

Thanks to my father's money and my mother's good taste I passed my childhood like the classic spoiled child, doing poorly in my studies and generally not accomplishing a blessed thing.

But how could it have been otherwise?

My father, who was afraid I would die on him, thirsted for sons for the continuity of the family line. Now he had got this rather delicate boy, so he postponed my education until it was too late. And my Provençal mother, as sweet as her compatriots, spared me every weariness, exertion, or pain.

Imagine the result.

Precisely because they loved me so much my parents connived to make of me, their own child, a "landslide"—as the Italians say today, meaning a disaster.

I have to say disaster when I think of what they had in mind.

My father wanted me to go into business. And with the lazy life I had been leading I certainly had no wish to wear myself out in the warehouses or on the streets.

My mother. What did my mother want? I do not even know what she wanted. She only wanted me in the house with her. She wanted me to sing with her and be a good little boy.

Not even she knew what a good little boy was.

What I can tell you is that she doted on me, very much, and on this point we always got along very well together.

But in a house like ours what can you do but dote? Good taste was in evidence everywhere, money was the main concern, and all hopes were on me. And I did not know how to do a thing.

No, that is not true. I did know how to do something. Sing, dress up, and have parties.

I had begun to make friends at Assisi, and my teen years began to unfold in a culture where singing was everybody's ambition and dressing up everybody's favorite pastime. And as I scarcely wanted for brocade, neither did I lack friends. I was king.

Bit by bit I grew up, and family plans expanded right along with me. My father's everlasting refrain, that I would be joining him in the mercantile calling, was now sung in counterpoint with something else—something that interested many of the "fine families" of that time—the use of arms and a life in the military.

Oh, I do not mean to suggest that the young men of Assisi were trying to get themselves killed in battle. Weapons were glory, an easy life, and prestige.

Assisi was a little town at the foot of a hill between Perugia and Spoleto. It did not need any weapons.

But arms were all the rage. People loved shining armor and horses in fancy trappings. No, these fine young men never failed to return from battle. The death of an upper- or middle-class citizen, under arms for fashion's sake, was never a very serious possibility.

They returned for May Day, and how their armor shone in the parade! Ah, the ladies were even more enthusiastic than their men when it came to armor.

Those who did not return were the poor wretches dragged from prison for the occasion and told to go fight. They were always the simple, the gullible, and they lumbered to the fray with nothing but a short sword, driven on by their great habituation to suffering.

By now it was clear that I was not cut out to be a businessman. Even my mother agreed with me, and had warded off my father's last broadsides. Defeated now in the dreams he had for me, he had sunk into the preoccupations of his warehouse, which was doing a brisk business.

Now pieces of armor began to appear here and there in the house, swords, breastplates—things like that.

The project received a timely fillip from the jumbled political situation.

Lothar, one of the Counts di Segni, had ascended the papal throne under the name of Innocent III. Three months later, just in the spring of 1198, the Àssisans had assaulted the Fortress of the Rock, symbol of the imperial might. And they had destroyed it.

Now matters grew more serious. Perugia prepared a lesson for the boldness of Assisi.

And indeed the lesson turned out badly for Assisi. We were overcome.

I say "we." Yes, I, too, was there, in the battle, driven by my whole circle of friends, who idolized me in my shining breastplate, and by my mother's smile.

My father had frowned at me, and had only said, "Take care. You have no principles. You are a dreamer."

I surely took care.

I crossed swords with no one at Collestrada, where the encounter with the Perugians took place, and I ended up where you always end up if you do not grasp war maneuvers very well—as a prisoner.

I was not very happy about that, even though basically I had done what my father had told me to do. I had taken care.

But my sense of glory had received a slap.

Prisoner. What a humiliation.

During my year in captivity at Perugia, I came to realize that war was not precisely my cup of tea. But I was unable to decide what to do with my life instead.

What was left for me if I did not wish to go into business, and if arms—the real kind, the kind that draw blood—were not for a dreamer the likes of me?

It was a sad year. The prison was not a nice place, in spite of the fact that my family managed to get messages and food packages through to me, thanks to friends in Perugia.

I fell ill.

I passed my days, and nights, in thought. I lived within myself, plunged into the abyss of my poverty-stricken reality, and I drowned in melancholy.

Never had I been so sad. I think my illness was actually due to the sadness.

Later I knew joy, the true joy of being alive. But I must say that for the moment I was tasting all the depression of a young person clutching his or her head in desperation and not knowing what decision to make.

It can kill!

I felt myself suffocating!

The explosive charge of life that I contained was covered over with a thick scab of doubt—un-faith, un-hope, and un-love.

I must have made the Perugians sorry for me by my silence and my lifeless look. In any case they were persuaded to allow me to depart for Assisi. Doubtless they said to one another, "This poor little lad will never be a danger to our city!"

What a fuss my mother made! I think she was so happy to have me home with her that she was glad I was sick.

Ah, mothers!

My mother's attentions, along with the sunshine of Assisi,

little by little gained the upper hand, and I was on the road to health once more.

Once I had begun to regain my health I noticed I had changed—changed a great deal.

Sorrow had broken the soil, where a bad upbringing, based on permissiveness and weakness, had only hardened the ground.

I realized that my long illness had actually been a grace.

It had acted as a plow, turning over the earth, breaking it up, and letting the season of spring burst out.

Above all it had done two great things for me. It had deprived me of my security, and it had given me new eyes.

As for my security, it had really taken it away, making me taste the bitter poverty of the little, weak, insecure, sick person, who can find the path of truth and love only in humility. But what was most important to me was the new way in which my eyes saw everything.

I had the impression that I had never seen a single thing before, and I understood what the psalm meant, "They have eyes, but never see" (Ps. 115:5).

I had not seen!

Yes, now I saw the sun, the moon, the earth, the springs, the flowers. I had not seen them before.

They had passed me by, taken for granted. They might as well have been landscape. I had merely gaped at them, as one gapes at strangers.

But now they spoke to me, I felt them near, I loved them, they moved me.

In fact I did not cease to weep when I beheld a sunset, or the meadows covered with poppies and lilies.

Everything seemed new to me, ever new, and as light entered my eyes it transformed itself into joy within my heart.

I think my first real prayers were said at that time, although I had prayed with my mother so often before. In any case, I am sure my need to give thanks dates from that time.

Thanks to the sky.

Thanks to the earth.

Thanks to life.

Thanks to God.

God!

Who was God for me?

Oh, it is difficult to answer that.

I, Francis, child of this Umbrian countryside, had inhaled God with all my tribe from time immemorial. I had identified God with the tenderness of our olive trees, with the beauty of our stupendous landscape, with the light that spread everywhere and suffused everything it reached.

How can one be born in a land so lovely and so harmonious, and take no notice of God behind it all?

No, it cannot be done. My compatriots believed in God and so did I.

But what was God for us?

What was God for me?

It is difficult to answer.

And so all I can tell you simply and clearly is that whatever God had been for me now burst upon me from without.

The "someone" that God was, so far away, whom I had known from my Umbrian childhood, was becoming someone very near and was beginning to speak to me with all the wonderful signs God placed in the sky and on the earth that we call creatures.

I began to grasp that God was all around me, and had sent those marvelous messengers, creatures, before his face.

I felt that he wished to speak to me. So I kept repeating, "What do you want me to do, Lord?"

This phrase came to my lips with ever greater ease, and later in Spoleto, in that last wretched effort to send me off to the military, when I was asking help of heaven in making a decision, I used it as the response I gave to the voice that kept asking, "Francis, which do you choose, the servant or the master?" "The master," I would reply, and add, "What do you want me to do, Lord?"

It Is the Poor One
Who Saves

Middle-class rich boy that I was, I never would have thought that it would be the poor who would be my salvation.

Owing to the upbringing I had received at my mother's hands, as well as the attitude of the church I had been attending up until that time, I had always thought that it was we rich and well-to-do who would be the ones to rescue the poor. The latter depended on us, it seemed, and our generosity was their salvation. Without us they would have been destined to death.

What blindness was ours and mine!

The truth was just the contrary, and now life was demonstrating this to me.

It was the poor who would be my salvation, and not I theirs.

It was they who would put me back on my feet.

After my long illness, which as I have already told you had given me new eyes, the poor had entered my life massively. They were involving me, educating me.

And I saw them everywhere—on the steps of the churches, at the doors of the houses, all over the streets, in the shelters, in the haylofts, in town, in the country, everywhere.

Stop to think that in my time there were no retirement plans for the elderly, and social welfare was still a dream to come. The conclusions are easy to draw.

The moment a laborer ceased working, whether from illness or old age, he was on the sidewalk.

The number of beggars was multiplying ad infinitum, and society was infected by a plague that neither state nor Church had the wherewithal to overcome: the plague of misery.

The poor were at the mercy of the public alms, and of the constant activity of good Christians.

Queens and the rich vaunted themselves on their dedication to the alleviation of poverty, and noble families found in the poor a visible opportunity for the expression of their generosity, paternalism, or, on occasion, authentic charity.

No country dwelling was without a corner of the hayloft reserved to the wandering beggar. No Christian lady neglected to set aside a bit of bread and soup for those who sought alms to survive in the name of Christ.

My mother, too, was generous with the poor, and gave them many things. I had always seen many poor in my home.

But as I have told you, when I began to live again, and to see everything with new eyes, I saw the poor with new eyes as well.

In fact it was most of all the poor that I saw with new eyes.

I must tell you that it was just precisely they who saved me, who drew me out of the cavern of my selfishness.

It was in seeing them that I found strength to live, for I found in them my tomorrow, my vocation, the joy of doing something worthwhile with my life.

To boot, the poor educated me to the patience I lacked, to the penance of which I was so ignorant.

Not to mention docility, graciousness in accepting from others, hope in tomorrow, and courage to go on!

But most of all they opened my heart to understand something. No, I shall not tell you yet. I shall tell you later—the name of someone they led me to discover. Wait a little.

℘

The discovery of the poor led me to become an arrant thief—abetted in this proposition by my native impulsiveness and my rather childish radicalism.

Theft had become my favorite pastime. I shall not attempt to tell you how many things I stole from my house during that period!

No drawer, no remnant, was safe any longer. I found, I cut, I disappeared.

I returned with more joy in my heart every time—and with less and less fear of a scolding from my parents.

Of course!

My mother let me do as I pleased. My father was somewhat more strict with me. Especially when he began to realize what a bad turn his son Francis had taken (he declared him to be "unprincipled," and yes, a bit disturbed), he began to look well to his warehouse!

The first time I caused my father to lose his mind was when I had decided not to go into business with him as he wanted; now, the second time, and this was a bit more serious, was when I stole from his shop.

We butted heads. I overdid things, I was a wastrel, while he was greedy and hard. I am sorry to say he was conceiving a real antipathy for me. This state of affairs disturbed a mother who was so sweet, who straightway closed her eyes to my thievery, and who kept telling my father, "Be patient, let him alone, he is still not well."

But I was well. I was well, and how well I was!

Never had I felt as well as I felt now, now that I had found the law of reciprocal containers, and now that I would have sold all Assisi in order to help the poor.

The law of reciprocal containers? Ah, you would like to know what that is? Well, the law of reciprocal containers is the first thing you learn when you begin to notice the poverty around you.

Find it where it is and put it where it isn't.

It is such an easy rule, and it should be the rule of the politicians at all levels of government, but . . .

A child such as I was makes mistakes in the implementation of this law. I stole, very simply, thinking that that was how it was done. I saw no reason for carrying the Code of Canon Law around with me. But . . .

Things were viewed somewhat differently by grownups such as my father.

I have to say that it was not my nature to conform. And my father was too prideful to consider the slightest possibility that his son had gone mad.

Yes, my manner of action had caused a number of people to think that I had gone out of my mind.

And this was what really exasperated my father. More than my generosity wounded his avarice, his neighbors' little smiles wounded his pride. Their knowing looks had begun to insinuate that Francis, son of Peter di Bernardone, had gone insane. They believed it, too. If you seriously set yourself to follow Christ and the Gospel, people (especially churchgoers, who have solved all their conscience problems by placing themselves midway between heaven and earth, between enjoying what is "down here" and storing up security "up there")—people will tell you you are crazy, the moment you distance yourself from their manner of living.

As if all this were not enough, in the heat of my enthusiasm I had taken to dressing in tatters—so that I began to be laughed at behind my back, and I even had a few stones tossed at me, as if I had departed from the common thinking and now had begun to be refuted by the community of "sensible people." Yes, if my father came to the point of hailing me before the Bishop it was not because of his money. It was because he was afraid of how he was beginning to look to the people of Assisi, of whom he took such great account.

As we had now gone public with the matter, I told my side of the story too, and the Lord inspired me to make a cruel, but evangelical and clear, gesture.

I stripped naked, and flung my garments (which were his, of course) into the arms of my father. "From this moment forth I am no longer Francis, son of Peter di Bernardone, but Francis, child of God!"

Oh, boy, were we something.

I realized I had been cruel toward my father, but I felt too that the Gospel was not being lived, and that people were making a joke out of something very cruelly real—the poor.

Yes, I had been cruel. But I was young, immature, and my poverty was still in its early stages—what you call "social justice."

Basically I was giving the middle class a slap in the face. My poor garments said, "Don't you see that it is you who are the thieves? That it is you who reduce your fellow citizens to poverty? You, Peter di Bernardone, you have grown rich only by squeezing the last drop of sweat out of your workers, and you live and thrive on the tears of those who worked for you before and who now, unemployed and enfeebled, lie begging alms on the steps of the churches of Assisi."

How genuine, how authentic I felt, standing there naked before the Bishop!

I still ask myself today where I got the strength to make a gesture like that, a true sign that I had broken with hypocrisy, and with the rhetoric of those who were considered "good."

I do not know whether it was for modesty or for love, but the Bishop covered me with his mantle.

For love, I think. In any case he liked me, and sought to understand me.

What I am sure of is that in that moment I felt I represented all the poor in the Church of the poor, and I had the impression that until then that mantle had been a little cold—perhaps because it was too rich, and weighted down with things that had no use.

A God Who Is Poor

Now that I had scales on my eyes no longer, and had begun to see creatures in their astounding beauty, and the poor in their liberating suffering, I felt the need of silence and prayer.

The outskirts of Assisi held no dearth of places to pray in solitude, and whether I climbed Subasio, covered with its great woods, or descended toward Twisting Brook in the meadows, it was no difficult matter to be at my ease, all alone to pray and to weep.

I had donned the garb of a hermit. It gave me a sense of detachment and full freedom, and I loved to run barefoot in the fields, with a bodily joy which God had begun to sow within me now.

It was the fall of the year 1205, and the leaves of the oaks, ashes, poplars, and alders were russet and bright yellow, and spoke to me overwhelmingly of how I had been born in a land of astonishing loveliness, made just to adore God— whom I now began to call "my Most High Lord."

Below, not far from Twisting Brook, there was one place particularly dear to me. There in a lovely glade, surrounded by meadow, was a fascinating little church. It was poor, constructed of unhewn stone, and utterly quiet. Its name was

Saint Damian, and it seemed made for me, as my taste ran
not just to poor people but to poor churches.

I made my first retreats there, and as I sat, or knelt on the
floor, praying, in that little church, I could see the considerable chinks in the wall and the holes in the roof. The church
was gradually crumbling down.

But in the Gothic arch over the altar was a marvelous
wooden crucifix, Byzantine in style; and what spoke to me,
what pleased me about it, was Jesus' so royal regard—especially the look in that pair of extraordinarily humble and
tender eyes.

I passed hours in gazing, praying, and weeping.

I wept so much I grew ashamed. I would say to myself,
"Francis, you are a baby."

But I continued to weep, and the tears were good for me.

One day as I gazed at the crucifix I had the altogether
clear impression that the lips were moving. At the same moment I heard a voice: "Francis, repair my house! You can see,
it is all in ruins."*

---

*Oh, I do hope you don't get all hung up on the thing about the lips I saw
moving and the voice my ears heard. Now that I understand such matters
a little better I can tell you about them, and it will help you not to become
fanatic or superstitious but to accept everything in a spirit of faith.

In reality, the lips of a Christ of wood do not move. If my father, for
instance, Peter di Bernardone, had been standing next to me at that moment,
being so rich and having such good sense, he would not have seen a thing, and
especially, he would not have heard a thing.

It was I who did the seeing and the hearing, for I saw and heard in faith.
No one has ever been able to explain how this phenomenon, on the border-
line between the human and the divine, actually occurs. What is known is that
it takes place entirely in the realm of faith, hope, and love, and that it is utterly
personal.

God clothes our faith with vision, with light, with voice, in order to come
to the aid of our poverty and to give clarity to our relationship with him. But
the relationship itself has all its validity in faith.

It was in faith that Abraham saw the angel, that Jacob saw the ladder that
reached to heaven. It was in hope that Moses saw the burning bush, and in
love that Joseph interpreted the dream that he should take Mary as his spouse.

I shall not attempt to convey the effect this had upon me. It was like a message linking me to the invisible world, and it sealed a long period of wavering, of enthusiasm, and of searching.

I felt permeated by an infinite sweetness, and I went up to the crucifix to kiss it.

I was all alone, and I was not afraid to leap up on the altar to embrace Jesus with my whole self.

I do not know how long I stayed there, touching, stroking, caressing, and contemplating Christ.

Every so often, amid tears and sighs I kissed him, now upon the hands, now upon the wounds in his feet and side, and my hand tenderly stroked him, like someone passionately in love.

I must confess that in that moment I was thunderstruck at the mystery of Christ's incarnation.

Just as it had been the poor who had been my inspiration to "rise and walk," so now it was the idea of the incarnation of God which was becoming my only answer to all the whys I had posed myself up to that time in my life.

Jesus was the epitome of all: in him heaven and earth resolved all their contradictions in one stupendous, vital act of divine unification, and satisfied all the thirsts of humanity.

From that instant at Saint Damian I felt actualized in Christ, understood, interpreted—and most of all, happy.

Jesus' cross was humanity's happiness, love's answer to all the whys, the resolution of every conflict, the overcoming of every tension and polarization, God's victory over death.

If the Son of God had died on the cross, I was saved.

But as far as externals are concerned, nothing visible happens.

When Bernadette saw the Blessed Virgin in the grotto at Lourdes, there were thousands of people around her who did not see anything at all.

What counts—what gives value to our relationship with the divine—is the instrument by which God speaks to a human being: faith.

All sadness would have to be banished.

Every one of us was lord of the world.

Every pauper was rich.

Every heart was satiated.

Every project was possible.

I clambered down from the altar and began to dance, barefoot, on the floor of the Church of Saint Damian.

I felt like a clown, crazy with joy and life.

I sang, I laughed, I wept, I rolled about on the floor, as if the divine eagle had wounded my heart and I could no longer contain the gladness that gushed up from this seizure of love.

I do not know how long I remained in this state. I was beside myself with joy. I do know that at a certain moment I found myself standing before a chink in the wall, about the size of my hand, and I recalled the words Jesus had said to me: "*Francis, repair my house.*"

I am no stonemason, in fact I had never done a blessed thing in my life, but I assure you that at that instant I felt capable of building a church as big as the Cathedral of Saint Rufinus.

And you think Saint Damian was going to be a problem?

I ran out of doors and began to gather stones, especially squarish ones.

But I had to pause very early in my work, for a workman came up behind me and shouted, "Hey, stones cost money! Those are mine! Get your own stones!"

The reproaches addressed to me for my old vice of thieving for the Lord did not succeed in dampening my joy, however. Gladness still gushed up within me, in fact it seemed to numb my hands, which, being so delicate, now appeared all grooved and creased from this toil devoid of calm or prudence.

So I decided to go to Assisi to beg stones.

My reputation for any seriousness, compromised for some

time now in any case, took a severe turn for the worse as I took up that collection.

Look at what Peter di Bernardone's boy has got into his head!

He has surely gone mad.

Yes, my friends of Assisi, I have gone mad.

But if you only knew my madness!

I am mad with love.

I can no longer help it.

I can no longer resist.

If I but look into that Jesus' eyes, I am on fire right down to my insides.

Do you not know that my Most High Lord is God's Son?

And do you not know that he became a human being, and as if that had not been enough, a poor person? And how poor he became!

Just see how poor he is. He has nothing left at all.

He, the creator of heaven and earth, has himself come among us.

He did not send someone else, he came himself!

He did nothing to get himself accepted in high places, nor did he bring anything along to make himself more comfortable.

He did not hide behind the wall of his might and his divinity; he accepted life as the last and least of us.

He was God and he became the poor one among us, the weak one, the wounded one, the calumniated one, the imprisoned one, the condemned one!

Have compassion, people of Assisi, give me a few stones. I have to fix up God's church!

Then I ran and ran to Saint Damian.

I could no longer keep away from that place, from that crucifix!

I decided to live there, to be there always, and live by alms and work.

I asked the priest who held services in that church never to allow the lamp before the crucifix to go out, and I undertook to keep it supplied with oil myself.

I felt I could have burned my blood, and I would have shed it gladly to see the lamp burning before that crucifix—which had explained to me the mystery of the whole universe, and which had helped me to enter into the truth of Christ and of things invisible.

The Mystery of Poverty

The crucifix of Saint Damian had revealed to me something very important, something I tried not to forget. In fact it had become the standard and guide of my life.

Poverty did not consist in helping the poor, it consisted in being poor.

Helping the poor was basic. It was basic to charity, and an expression of charity. But being poor was something else.

Jesus had been poor.

I, Francis, wished to be poor.

What it meant to be poor I began to see very clearly. All I had to do was look at the poor or look at Jesus.

Being poor meant having nothing, or almost nothing. It meant not possessing wealth, not possessing things, not possessing money, not possessing security, just like the poor, just like Jesus. And even this was not everything. Even this was but the external, visible sign of poverty.

True poverty went to the bottom of things, and touched the spirit. For Jesus had said, "Blessed are the poor in spirit, theirs is the kingdom of heaven" (Matt. 5:3).

How these words captivated me! How I sought to grasp their meaning!

Blessed are the poor in spirit!

That meant that not all the poor were equal. That meant that there were those who were poor in spirit, and there were those who were just poor.

And when I thought of the poor I had met in my life, especially in recent years, it was clear that there were poor who were only poor—very sad, often angry, and certainly not blessed.

And then again, I recalled very well, there were poor people who were quite otherwise, poor people who wore their poverty beautifully.

Poor people who had the conviction that they were being guided by God, supported by his Presence.

Poor people who were able to love, in spite of their sudden vexations—poor people who were patient in trial, rich in hope, strong in adversity.

Poor people who were blessed because they could bear witness, every day, that God was present in their lives, and that he provided for them as he did for the sparrows of the sky, which possess no granaries.

Yes, this captivated me.

To bear witness, to testify, to myself and to other human beings, that God alone sufficed for me, and that I did not have to be concerned about anything, anything at all—"think of the flowers of the field; they never have to spin or weave; yet not even Solomon in all his regalia was like one of these" (Luke 12:27).

The thought of being fed, clothed, and guided by God himself uplifted me. No power on earth could have persuaded me to change my mind. Putting a little money aside—keeping a larder—buying a house—for me this would have meant a lack of trust in my Lord.

Oh, I would not have proposed this manner of life for everyone. For example, it would not have been the thing for my father.

That would have been impossible. Society had other laws. People had different callings.

I was proposing it for myself, as I wished to be a witness of God's love. And I would have proposed it for those who would follow me.

Yes, for some time now I had begun to consider, and desire, being followed in this manner of life. I began to dream of having companions, with whom to share faith and sing praises to my Most High Lord; and he would truly be the Lord of our life.

This is how I regarded the religious—the consecrated person, the person who had abandoned all things simply to follow Jesus, to be a witness of the invisible God out on the streets of the world.

My choice to be poor, then, was not a social or political choice, but a mystical one.

There was no lack of social struggles in my time. There was plenty of popular protest against injustices. The country folk were in a continual struggle with the landowners, and free towns like Assisi were constantly on guard against the interference of the feudal ones, against being overpowered by the great cities.

It was right to do this, and people did it.

People have been involved in the struggle for liberation since Adam, and the struggle is never over. It is an obligation on the part of each human being in simple justice, not to mention the perfection of truth and love.

But blessedness was another matter.

When I, Francis, heard the call of the Gospel, I did not set about organizing a political pressure-group in Assisi. What I did, I remember very well, I did for love, without expecting anything in return; I did it for the Gospel, without placing myself at odds with the rich, without squabbling with those who preferred to remain rich. And I certainly did it without any class hatred.

I did not challenge the poor people who came with me to fight for their rights, or win salary increases. I only told them that we would be blessed—if also battered, persecuted, or killed. The Gospel taught me to place the emphasis on the mystery of the human being more than on the duty of the human being.

I did not understand duty very well. But how well I understood—precisely because I had come from a life of pleasure—that when a poor person, a suffering person, a sick person, could smile, that was the perfect sign that God existed, and that he was helping the poor person in his or her difficulties.

The social struggle in my day was very lively and intense, almost, I should say, as much so as in your own times. Everywhere there arose groups of men and women professing poverty and preaching poverty in the Church and the renewal of society. But nothing changed, because these people did not change hearts.

When poor persons are agitators, and their agitating succeeds, and they become rich, they grow arrogant like the rest of the rich, and forget their old companions in misery.

This is what happened then, and this is what is happening among you.

Revolutionaries battle for the freedom of the working classes. But then they come to power, become wealthy, and shoot down the rest of the working class, who think differently from themselves. And then the others feel exploited, taken advantage of.

And what of the union organizers in the rich countries, who are the most intransigeant of all in refusing to allow the working people of poor countries to share the common bread?

No, brothers and sisters, it is not enough to change laws. You have to change hearts. Otherwise, when you have completed the journey of your social labors you shall find yourselves right back at the beginning—only this time it is you who will be the arrogant, the rich, and the exploiters of the poor.

This is why I took the Gospel path. For me the Gospel was the sign of liberation, yes, but of true liberation, the liberation of hearts. This was the thrust that lifted me out of the middle-class spirit, which is present to every age, and is known as selfishness, arrogance, pride, sensuality, idolatry, and slavery.

I knew something about all that.

I knew what it meant to be rich, I knew the danger flowing from a life of easy pleasure, and when I heard the text in Luke, "Alas for you, who are rich," my flesh crept. I understood. I had run a mortal risk, by according a value to the idols that filled my house, for they would have cast me in irons had I not fled.

It is not that I did not understand the importance of the various tasks that keep a city running. I understood, but I sought to go beyond.

You can reproach me, go ahead. But I saw, in the Gospel, a road beyond, a path that transcended all cultures, all human constructs, all civilization and conventions.

I felt the Gospel to be eternal; I felt politics and culture, including Christian culture, to be in time.

I was made always to go beyond time.

In the quest for justice and human equality, the Old Testament would have been enough. It would have sufficed to read Deuteronomy, Kings, Leviticus.

There, one is taught to build the State along the lines of good sense, and the old theocratic mentality.

There one learns to make war, to take captives, to divide booty, to kill, to torture—and all this in the name of God, just as was sometimes done in my day, and is sometimes done in yours.

But the Gospel was another matter.

The Gospel is the insanity of a God who is always losing, who gets himself crucified to save humanity.

The Gospel is the madness of people who, in the midst of tears, need, and persecution, still cry out that they are blessed.

I had grasped all this, and I understood why the wise and the well-balanced would have destroyed me. So I appealed to insanity in order to save myself. And I was happy to have found the true madness, the saving madness of the Gospel.

⚘

But there was more. God explained it to me by causing me to meet a leper.

What a horror I had of lepers!

Perhaps it was an attitude I had picked up in church, where lepers were cited as an image of sin. Or perhaps it was on account of their forced isolation. Or perhaps it was because people were afraid of catching leprosy from them. Whatever the reason, the fact is that I could not bear the sight of a leper, and would not have dared touch one for all the gold in the world.

Whenever I imagined that I might meet one some day, I banished the thought straightaway.

But I met one anyway.

And the street was so narrow that I practically had to bump into him—unless I had run away. I certainly felt like doing that.

Oh, how I felt like it. But the memory of the crucifix of Saint Damian blocked my escape.

I froze in the middle of the street.

The leper was coming toward me, very slowly, all in tatters.

He held his hands clasped toward me, and fixed me with a look of sweetness and sorrowful humility.

That was when I remembered the crucifix of Saint Damian. It seemed to me that it was the same eyes that were looking at me.

Then I do not really know what came over me.

I leapt forward and embraced the leper, and kissed him on the mouth.

He began to weep. And so did I, with him.

I pulled out everything I had in my pockets and gave it to him. But it was nothing compared with what he had given me, with what he had made me see in that moment and in that kiss.

I had touched the wondrous garment of her whom I was to espouse forever: my Lady Poverty!

I had contemplated in his eyes the mystery of the Incarnation of the Word.

Now I knew my spouse. In her I could feel myself to be in love with the one God himself loves: the poor person.

My Lady Poverty, whom I had seen in the leper, was the poverty of the entire world, she was in solidarity with all that is little, weak, and suffering, she was the tender focal point of the mercy of God.

My Lady Poverty!

Her most humble visage was the face of all the poor I had ever met, and who had gazed upon me with sweetness and infinite discretion.

Her eyes were pearls washed in tears, but filled with a mystery not revealed to many.

Her afflicted members had the transparency of light, and were the only members truly chaste, and worthy to embrace the very Christ.

Her perfume was the odor of things invisible, and invited one not to the *eros* of easy things, but to the *agape* of heroes of the spirit.

Until now I had thought of poverty as the curse of the earth, a fearful mistake in creation, a kind of forgetfulness on the part of God, an inexpressible chaos which swallowed human beings and made them suffer.

Now I saw something else!

The curse was not in poverty, it was in wealth. It was in power, which hardened and poisoned hearts.

Poverty was not creation's mistake but its last page, perhaps the most important page, the one that placed men and women before mystery, and obliged them to seek after God and the supreme gift of self.

It was not God's forgetfulness of us, but his true, raw way of digging out of the depths of us free love and naked faith.

It was not chaos, clutching at men's and women's throats to make them cry out and curse the day they were born, but the motherly lap that would give them birth, bear them to the Kingdom.

From that moment I had no more doubts: Poverty was the dwelling place of the divine, the highest school of true love, the mighty pull of mercy, the encounter with God made easy, the surest way to cross this earth.

I espoused my Lady Poverty in desire, and from that moment all fear died within me.

Or rather, true freedom began.

❧

I should not like to be anyone's cause of suffering, even unintentionally, especially, in this case, the most generous.

If I insist on the blessedness of the poverty the Gospel proclaims, it is not in order to enter into any polemic with those who, also in the name of the Gospel, wage a guerrilla war to bring about a change when the poor are beaten, starved, tortured, and humiliated.

I admire Camilo Torres, I admire Che Guevara. I admire all Christians who have chosen death with courage, to defend the poor.

They were not the first, nor shall they be the last, for, throughout history, so-called just wars have always been proposed to satisfy people's thirst for justice.

Even Saint Thomas speaks of the possibility of having to face a "just war."

In my time, the Crusade against the Muslims was considered a "just war," and the Church itself promoted it.

In your times, you consider as just, very just, guerrilla wars waged against totalitarian regimes, against dictatorships which oppress the poor.

Perhaps the Crusaders were right in my time. Just think of the Battle of Lepanto. And perhaps the guerrillas of today are right.

I am not debating, and above all I am not judging.

I am only saying that there is another method of combating and vanquishing, that of nonviolence. And I am pointing out that in the Gospel it undoubtedly has the primacy. And I, Francis, consider it more effective as well, even though it may be more difficult.

The struggle against injustices and outrages, especially those committed against the poor and defenseless, is basic Christianity, and Christians are not permitted to be silent, to withdraw, to refuse to get involved.

If they understood, really understood, they would volunteer to die for justice.

That is what Jesus did.

But nowhere is it written that to make your adversary yield it is necessary or indispensable to employ the sword, the machine gun, or the tank.

The highest claim of the Gospel is that I can cause my enemy to yield with my unarmed love, with my bare hand, as Gandhi did, as Martin Luther King did, as all who believe in nonviolence do, as Bishop Romero did in your times.

What a sublime example this unarmed person gave! What wonderful words he spoke against the arrogant, who massacre his people!

Give a nation a handful of men and women like that—give

the Church a band of heroes of strength like that—and then you will realize that when Jesus proposed nonviolence he was not doing so in order to lose battles. He was doing so in order to win them, and win them in the only way worthy of a human being: without shedding the blood of others, but by shedding one's own.

This is the principle of martyrdom, which has never been lacking in the Church and which is the highest witness a human being can bear upon earth.

Further than that one cannot go.

The Merry Company

I had never entertained the slightest thought of living alone.
Anytime I heard anyone predict the hermit's life for me,
because I fled populated areas after my first conversion, or
because I had donned a hermit's dress in order to gain a
sense of freedom, I knew they were mistaken.

I was made for companions, I was made for community.

Every man I passed by, I looked at as a potential companion on my journey, especially if he was young, poor, and
knew how to pray.

From the very beginning of my conversion to God, I
sensed that there would be many to follow me one day. The
road I had found was too beautiful, the joy that the Gospel
of Jesus gave me was too beautiful.

Religion in my day was badly lived. Parishes were only half
alive, and were for the most part places of cult rather than of
life.

Priests in their sermons sought to terrify people with the
usual discourses on eternal punishment, while the Gospel
was buried in a heavy and inexorably clerical tradition. There
was no room for the laity, married people, country folk.
Only religious counted.

Above all, joy was missing. To be Christian meant to be

sad—especially for women, who stifled their femininity in a thousand fears. True, at carnival time the end of the world erupted, in reaction. But this exaggeration was a sign precisely of a repressive culture and an unripe faith.

And yet, people were so rich in goodness, so thirsty for God!

At the drop of a hat, a young person would head straight for the religious life!

I had scarcely embarked upon the path of the Gospel, expressing it as a liberation, when companions surged toward me like waves of the sea.

Bernard da Quintavalle, Peter Cattani, Egidio, Philip, Masseo, Leo, Rufinus, Pacificus, Silvester!

How many memories!

What sweetness in the thought of my companions in faith!

They astounded and enchanted me.

They astounded me that they would have confidence in me, poor, ignorant Francis, and they enchanted me by their simplicity and enthusiasm.

They seemed to be madmen. Whenever we met, we would run in the meadows like little boys, singing, drunk with the gladness of the Gospel.

We had found happiness just in being together, in the power of feeling ourselves to be Church.

One would have said we had just been released from prison. And we had been—from the prison of our past, of our complexes, of our groundless fears. From the start we had agreed to live just as the Gospel invites one to, without adding anything of our own.

And so when we had a decision to make, we would open the Gospel at random, after having said a little prayer, and then we did whatever was written, without adding anything.

This manner of action gave us a boundless liberty, and nurtured simplicity of heart with some solid food.

Another important element taking shape in the community we were forming was the primacy of faith instead of structures.

We felt ourselves to be a community in search of God, not a seminary for the priesthood.

What made us one was Christ, and the imitation of him gave meaning to the manner of living of each one of us.

There was the whole expression around us of the life of a simple Christian. There was the man from the country and there was the scholar, there was the laborer and there were those who like Bernard da Quintavalle who had to abandon a great deal of wealth to enter our Order.

There were priests, too, like Silvester or Leo. But this did not make anyone feel he was any less a member of the community than they.

On the contrary, I must say that the desire of most of us was to remain simple brothers, for the dignity of the priesthood was feared as a danger to humility, to unobtrusiveness, to the desire to count for nothing.

Now we were members of the poor class, the lowest class, and the brothers truly wished to remain such.

At first we took up residence in a pair of lean-tos we had discovered down by Twisting Brook, which served as a shelter for donkeys.

But that did not last long.

A farmer soon came with a donkey.

He was unhappy with us, and made us move out because we had taken the animal's space. And perhaps we were bothering him.

So we headed for the woods around Saint Mary of the Angels, the little church, originally called the Portiuncula, right in the middle of the woods, so simple and solitary.[*]

---

[*]This name derives from *portiuncula terreni* (a small plot of land) where Benedictines long before Francis's time had lived. The little chapel is now enclosed in the Basilica.

There it was a simple matter to build a few huts for shelter.
We lived like skylarks.

Our real prayer was our gladness. Our rule was the Gospel, and the certainty that it was God who was guiding us.

When I think back on that time I feel uplifted. I would have liked to fasten forever onto that manner of living, for it helped us to break with all our habits, and immersed us in the utopia of the Gospel, which is an explosion of freedom, simplicity of life, love, and the absence of problems.

Unfortunately, things were not always like that. Later on we too knew complications—books, houses . . . houses . . . especially the houses, which we never finished building, and which weighed heavily upon the Gospel.

I had reason to suffer and be uneasy when I saw building in progress.

Once I outright set about to raze to the ground a little house that seemed too large to me, too deluxe for us who wished to be poor.

It was always a drama for me, a thorn planted in my heart.

Besides, in building, we turned aside from our original choice of following Jesus in his poverty, although we did not mean to. Our visible wealth was like a weed, suffocating the delicate shoot that contained the very presence of God.

The same good sense that usually characterized us was becoming a continual danger to our freedom to take the Kingdom by storm.

Pure love was the only thing that could discern what we really ought to do, and I have to say it was the maddest of us who saw most aright.

We were all pulled in two opposite directions—especially I, who bore the common responsibility.

We were drawn to silence, solitude, and prolonged prayer, of course.

We loved solitary places—abandoned churches, like Saint Damian, Saint Peter, Saint Mary of the Angels.

We would never have abandoned our hermitages so full of silence and peace, where just being with God became almost palpable.

We prayed a great deal.

But then too we were drawn to the proclamation of the Word to the poor, the missionary endeavor, the invitation of the Gospel to call human beings to penance and conversion.

What were we to do?

How were we to choose?

We held a great many discussions.

Then something happened.

I remember it as if it were yesterday. It was the twenty-fourth of February, 1208, the Feast of Saint Matthias.

As I was listening to the Gospel at Mass that day I was struck by the words Jesus addressed to the apostles as he sent them into the world.

No longer do I call you servants, but friends. For all that I have heard from the Father I have made known to you. It is not you who have chosen me—no, it is I who have chosen you, and have commissioned you to go and to bear fruit. And your fruit will remain, because whatever you ask of the Father in my name he will grant you.

From that moment forth, everything was clear. And lest there be any confusion, I doffed my hermit's garb and donned a cassock, tying it with a cord. And barefoot I went to preach penance, as the Gospel had indicated to me.

"Go and preach to all men and women."

Spring was approaching. We were jumping out of our skins.

The desire to announce to men and women the goodness of our Lord Jesus, and to share the good news of salvation with the poor, burned too hot within us for us to hold still.

We divided into groups of two, as the Gospel said, and off we set on the great adventure.

Egidio and I, Francis, took Market Street. Bernard da Quintavalle and Peter Cattani went the opposite way.

It will be superfluous to inform you that we had scheduled a rendezvous at the Portiuncula on our return. We loved each other too much, and we could not have stayed away from one another long, nor from the place where we had found felicity.

The journey was truly extraordinary.

I thought I saw the Church blossoming as I saw the meadows blossom around me.

I experienced in flesh and spirit the extraordinary words of Jesus:

"Do not worry about your life and what you are to eat, nor about your body and how you are to clothe it. Surely life means more than food, and the body more than clothing. Look at the birds in the sky. They do not sow or reap, or gather into barns; yet your heavenly Father feeds them" (Matt. 6:25-26).

And wherever we looked, what Jesus had said was true.

Indeed along all the paths we travelled, everything went just as Jesus had said it would.

Wherever we saw people, we paused, with great love, gladness, and peace, and asked whether they had need of any help. We worked in the fields, gratefully broke bread with the poor, and announced the Kingdom of God, seeking to spread hope and confidence.

People loved us, and we lacked nothing—not a single thing. We had solved the problem that most vexes human beings, and preoccupies them so: *the problem of tomorrow.*

We had done away with the fear of tomorrow.

"Each day has enough trouble of its own" (Matt. 6:34).

Saving something, putting it aside, piling it up—would have seemed to us like an insult to the God that led us by the hand, and who had promised to solve our problems himself, to provide for our needs himself: *"The Father himself feeds you."*

Finding a farmer who would invite us to supper and offer us the hayloft for the night was an enormous joy for us—the kind of joy you feel when you communicate in love with a brother or sister and discover, hour by hour, the help God is giving you.

It was victory over fear—the greatest sin against faith in a God of love.

Our preaching was simple, so simple. It did not take many words to say what we had to say.

"Be converted to the Gospel and do penance, for the Kingdom of God is near" (cf. Matt. 3:2).

When people had heard us they were no longer willing to let us leave them.

We traversed the whole of the March of Ancona. Then, as summer approached, we heard the call of the Portiuncula, and remembered the obligation of our fixed appointment.

No one failed to appear. Indeed our little group had grown by three, and among the three was Philip Longo.

There were eight of us now, and once again we settled down near the Church of Saint Mary of the Angels, in our huts, which we had constructed in the spring and which had stood up against the rains.

And so we finished the summer in the place we most loved. And we did not fail to remark how the people of Assisi were no longer afraid of us. They had begun to take us seriously. In fact they were actually helping us.

I was not displeased. And I saw my mother again, several times. She was at peace with me now, and often sent me provisions, which we distributed to the poor. There were very many poor in Assisi.

When autumn came we decided to set forth once more, driven by a desire to crystallize the experience we had had of the road; and we headed for the valley of the Rieti, stopping en route at Poggio Bustone.

I remember Poggio well. For two reasons.

At the time I was obsessed with the thought that God could scarcely be happy with my wicked past, and could not have forgiven me.

One night, while I was praying and weeping, I felt an infinite sweetness pervade me, all of me, and with it came the certitude that God had indeed forgiven me and that he loved me.

I was so happy that I roused my companions. I recounted everything to them, and I made a special effort to share with them the sweetness of that pardon.

It seemed to me then that I had the gift of prophecy. Yes, I prophesied.

I prophesied that our company would become many; and that we would always have to pardon absolutely everyone, seeing that God had pardoned us.

In the enthusiasm that ensued upon that day of peace and sweetness, we divided into four groups, and two by two we parted for the four quarters of the world.

Who could stop us?

We all met again, early in the year 1209, in our little branch-and-twig monastery of Saint Mary of the Angels. We had four new companions, and how glad we were to welcome them!

Now we were twelve. Now I was afraid. How could I manage to guide so many brothers?

I was happy, but at the same time I was concerned.

We took up residence at the Portiuncula, in that wood so hospitable, around that fantastic church that one needed but to enter to have the gift of prayer and tears.

The Portiuncula was owned by the Benedictine monks of Mount Subasio, and in my time it was said to have been constructed by pilgrims returning from the Holy Land.

It was dedicated to Mary.

There, when I closed my eyes and thought about my future, and the future of the order of brothers that was growing up around me, I realized that I had always considered this church to be the mother of all the churches that we had discovered, and in which we lived in order to pray to our God.

Yes, if it had been Saint Damian where I had grasped the mystery of the love of Jesus crucified, it was at Saint Mary of the Angels that my heart was filled with infinite tenderness toward the Virgin Mary, and a boundless confidence in her motherly intercession.

In my littleness, in which I sought to live in order to understand the Kingdom, I had the impression even then that, in order to be forgiven, it would have been enough simply to enter this place and pray.

Later, the Lord in his infinite goodness confirmed this.

What a pity that you have crowned this poverty and littleness with such a big dome!

And one more thing. Why have you destroyed that lovely wood?

How we loved to come there!

Now it is so much more difficult to see how everything was!

Clare, My Sister

Yes, companions had come, our Order had new members, and it seemed there would be many more. But what about women?

Or are ideals for men only?

The clearest thing in the world was that the ideals we had been discovering and living were above our strength, coarse and rough men as we were. But women would know how to live them!

Nonviolence, love of the poor, choosing the lowest place— it was they who were the experts. We knew this perfectly well.

We each had memories of women in our past—of sisters in our family, the playmates of our childhood, puppy love.

How many reveries, in all of us! Especially in myself, who had made my debut among my fellow human beings precisely as a singer and jester.

And so the image of woman was part and parcel of us, sons of this wondrous Umbrian soil, as sweetness, goodness, and delicacy.

Who among us was free of the repressed ideals of knighthood? Which of us had not sung on May Day for those flower-crowned playmates of ours at Assisi?

Such memories I had of women, I, Francis! And all beautiful memories and dear. But one stood out in my recollection above all the rest: Clare.

Clare was the daughter of Ortolana, a lady of the noble Offre-duzzi family.

She had two sisters, Catherine and Beatrice. They lived in a palace on Piazza San Rufino, which seemed more like a fortress than a home.

I had not seen her often, but I knew who she was. She would advance and recede on my horizon like a wondrous dream.

I was taken with her long hair, russet blonde—and her determined eyes.

I think she knew me, too. In Assisi we all knew one another, more or less, in spite of gratings and fences aplenty, and when I was converted to the Lord Jesus and began to hold the Gospel in my heart, I learned that she had set her mind on me and was seeking my aid.

She had always been good. She had not had my restless past. But she understood me, and now she was looking for me.

The times were not easy for serene and limpid encounters between a youth and a girl, but this was one encounter no one could have prevented.

It happened this way.

We met near Saint Damian, amid the meadows and the lilies, and Clare opened the conversation by astonishing me.

"Francis," she said, "I see that you are looking for God, and I should like you to help me."

"Clare," I responded, "my Most High Lord has summoned me to follow him, and peace is full within me. I should like to tell you a secret: I have espoused my Lady Poverty, and I propose to be faithful to her forever."

"And it is well that you have done so, Francis. No one but the Lady Poverty could make you happy, and I am content.

"I only ask you to help me. There is a great deal of talk in Assisi concerning the manner of life you and your companions lead at Saint Mary of the Angels.

"I, too, should like to live this life—the same life, the same prayer, and especially the same poverty.

"Francis, what ought I to do?

"Your rule I should like to make my own.

"And then too I have so many companions. They would follow me. They, too, are thirsty for God.

"Riches mean nothing to us any longer. Our days are too empty of meaning. We suffocate, in rhetoric and boredom.

"The time has come to cry out the Gospel, by means of our lives.

"Francis, think of us. Do not abandon us.

"Ask the Lord whether he wishes to have from us women as well, a pledge to leave all things to live the poverty of the Gospel and the charity of Jesus."

❧

Clare had received a solid spirit of religion from her mother; and from her father she had strength of character: it was not easy to tame Clare.

She had always been involved with the poor, she was not frivolous, and she was made for the Absolute that was God.

Speaking with her I felt a great succor in the depths of me.

God did the rest, and things were helped along by the relationship between Clare's family, the Offreduzzi, and Brother Rufinus, who stayed by my side and encouraged me in this new project.

In the company of Bona di Guelfuccio, her heart's friend, Clare began to frequent the chapel of the Portiuncula. And so we continued to meet.

Our conversation was always of our common ideals, as they ripened in me and in her.

It did not take me long to learn what breed of temper was in Clare.

I had never seen the like. In fact I came to see that in the matter of poverty she was more radical than I was. For the first time since my conversion I felt I had something solid, genuine, and reliable to lean on.

The preparation for her consecration was brief.

Clare was decisive in her proposal to abandon the world and "practice the Gospel to the letter," as we had put it ever since the same ideal had conquered us.

"Very well, then," I said to her.

"Poverty for you as well, daughter of knights!"

There was a great problem, however.

This was no question of entering a well-known, respected convent—an "ancient and approved order."

Clare was going to have to make her road alone, and inaugurate a form of the religious life on the advice of a poor fellow like me, Francis, whose only advantage was his great inexperience.

It would not be easy.

Clare had set the evening of Palm Sunday for her great step.

I had told her to dress for a feast day, and go to receive the palm from the hand of Bishop Guido, in the Cathedral at Mass.

Then . . .

Then what we were going to do should have gotten us all arrested. We must have been mad, completely crazy.

I still ask myself today how I could have brought myself to tell Clare to run away from home.

In the house of the Offreduzzi—as I have already told you, it was more of a fortress than a house—there were her brothers, armed to the teeth, and a very long way indeed from being ready to permit the most beautiful of their sisters to flee by night to a wood at Saint Mary of the Angels to enter a phantom monastery inhabited by the clowns we were considered to be.

And yet . . .

That night came, the night of Palm Sunday, in the year 1211.

Assisi slept under the moon. There in the house of the Offreduzzi someone was not sleeping, in fact was very busily engaged behind the only possible exit from the vestibules of the palace in the middle of the night: the door of the dead, that little door that every medieval house had for the purpose of discharging the coffins of the departed.

It was Clare, very, very slowly removing the timbers to open a passage to the street.

Outside, Pacifica di Guelfuccio, her brave friend, was waiting.

In silence the pair broke for the fields. I, Francis, with my companions, had lighted every lamp we could find at the Portiuncula, and awaited the fugitives.

Fra Rufinus and Fra Silvester had gone to meet them.

When the fugitives were in view we all went to meet them with lighted torches.

That procession in the night was something truly wondrous. It was a sign of most joyful hope in our poor life.

We did not as yet have a set ritual for the consecration of a virgin to God.

We did have a large pair of shears, however, which we kept as a sign of our desire to cut off everything at the shoulders for the Lord.

I can still see Clare's blonde head bending before me in the little church of Saint Mary of the Angels.

And all around, like glowing coals, everyone's shining eyes.

It was not easy to crop off that wonderful hair. It was easier to place over Clare's shoulders a sackcloth robe and provide a belt of cord and a pair of wooden clogs.

The ideal of poverty, accepted by woman, multiplied the strength of man, and rendered the beauty of the message universal.

❧

I still have to tell you about the hullaballoo that morning upon the discovery of Clare's empty chamber—of the fierce brothers' wild ride to Bastia, to the Convent of Saint Paul, which we had selected as Clare's temporary refuge, and of their entry into the church to win back their sister by force.

We heard about it afterward. Clinging to the altar in the face of her brothers' menacing advance, Clare had suddenly torn away her veil, and shown her assailants her shorn head.

The brothers retreated without a word. There was nothing you could do with someone like that.

Later, at Saint Damian, Saracens, too, would retreat before her glance.

They had attacked Assisi in armed bands. One night, a mob of irregulars had approached the convent. They found themselves before a woman, who, armed only with the ostensorium exhibiting the Eucharistic Body of the Lord, had placed herself there like an oak, in defense of those sisters of hers who had been committed to her motherly care.

Had they wished to enter the convent and work their will upon the sisters, they would have first have had to pass over her body.

This was Clare of Assisi.

❧

Strange. I have asked myself many times how it is possible that, in spite of personages as remarkable as Clare, as Catherine, as Teresa, you in the Church are still so antifeminist?

Yes, I have to say it, I, Francis. You are still antifeminist.

I cannot understand!

Have you fear of a woman because a woman endangers

your virtue? Or do you consider her, without openly saying so, as belonging to an inferior race, unworthy to touch the holy things?

But do you realize?

Now and then you even forbid her to ascend to the altar, reverently to read to the assembly a text of Scripture. Any man goes first. All he has to do is be a man.

Does this not seem to you to be exaggerating things?

Are you still the slaves of ancient cultures, in which a woman was of no account, in which she was subjugated by male arrogance and destined only to live behind a curtain like the women of the Muslims?

One would say that you have no prophecy, that you have no truth to proclaim. Above all one would say that you are still living in the past.

❧

The past is past and does not return.

It has taken two thousand years for the Gospel to begin to enter the hard necks of men who are externally Christian but who are stuck back in the circumcision. But now something is breaking through.

The Council has been a singular milestone in the transformation of the modern world, sweeping away a dead weight that burdened the Church.

And it could be this because, after so much suffering, the Gospel had penetrated to the very tips of its veins.

The political concept of the ancient theocratic state, in which we ourselves lived in the Middle Ages, where faith and culture, faith and politics, were one, is definitively superseded in the maturity of the Gospel, especially in these times of yours.

The juridicism of the ancients is submerged by the charity which conquers hearts.

The unconfessed racisms of caste have been reduced to

dust by the sense of equality announced and effectuated by the building of the Kingdom.

There is something new for women, too. Read carefully.

Today, a woman must hear the words of Jesus as a man hears them; and if Jesus says, "Go and make disciples of all nations," it must no longer be that a man hears this in one way and a woman in another.

❧

How you must re-think everything!

And how I would like to say to women of today, "Go!" with all the force of which my spirit is capable, and all my anxiety for the immense needs of a world athirst for the Gospel. This is an urgent invitation.

Transform your home into a convent—an ideal, spiritual one, as Saint Catherine did. Let prayer reign there, good counsel, and peace. Let your toil, wherever it is, be illumined by the power of your calling—for you were made to love, to comfort, to serve.

Do not copy men. Be authentic. Seek, in your femaleness, the root that distinguishes you from them. It is unmistakable, for it has been willed and created by God himself. Repeat to yourselves every day: A man is not a woman.

Waste no time in approaching men in order somehow to resemble them. Rather seek to remove yourselves as far as possible from their model. It is not yours, and it is rather marred and muddled even so.

I think there is a model for you women in the world. Mary of Nazareth.

It is scarcely possible that Jesus would not have thought of this during the thirty years of his earthly existence, or that he would not have sought to mold and shape a model for women.

Mary was so close to him!

And she was so attentive to him!

And she was altogether the Daughter of the Father, the Mother of the Word, the Spouse of the Spirit.

We have not yet sufficiently considered this exceptional woman.

We have not plumbed the depths of her reality as "woman of this earth," as our sister. We have not sufficiently considered her freedom, her autonomy, her self-fulfillment, day by day in her everyday life.

You women are going to have to be the ones to dig out something of the mystery of Mary, in prayer.

There has been too much sentimentality, and too much useless triumphalism! Especially coming from men. Especially if they are not married.

ℒ

And one more thing.

Do not let yourselves be guided by men any longer just because they are men. If you let them lead you do so because they are saints, and do not disdain the help of persons like Clare—who, though she is a woman, can tell you things of utility and power.

ℒ

Now, to give you a chance to relax a bit, I would like to recount a beautiful legend.*

Francis and Clare were walking together through the countryside, and it was white with snow. They came to a fork in the road near Saint Damian. Here the Master spoke up. "Now we should go our separate ways."

---

*Maria Sticco, S. Francesco d'Assisi (Edizioni O. R., Milan, 1975), pp. 146ff. And here I must insert a parenthesis. It is Maria Sticco, lovely Maria Sticco, who, with her book, has acquainted me with the heart of Francis more than anyone else.

It was ever he who pronounced the word of renunciation, which is strength.

And so Clare knelt on the snow, with all the alacrity and humility that came to her so spontaneously only in the presence of the Master, and awaited his blessing.

Then rising again, with her heart atremble like that of a sparrow in that white winter's desolation, she felt human desire force open her lips, and she asked like a little baby:

"Father, when shall we see one another again?"

"When the roses blow," Francis replied quickly, for he too was moved. But he had gone only a few steps when he heard once more the crystal voice of Clare, behind him:

"Father!"

Francis turned; and the brush at Clare's feet was a whole garden of flaming roses. And wherever the two saints cast their eyes, roses were blooming in the snow as if it had been May.

⚘

God grant that we may be able to see these same flowers along the pathway of our life. If we do, it will be a sign of the miracle God has accomplished in our hearts, enabling us to live the blessedness of chastity in the sweet daily conversation with woman—become in every way, like Clare, "our sister."

This Is Gladness

Whenever I climbed Mount Subasio in the sunshine I had the feeling that my whole body was penetrated by light—and along with the light, by joy.

At those moments as I walked along the path, I wondered how it could ever have been possible for me to feel down-hearted.

Gladness was within me, for it had vanquished me.

For me, sunlight was the creature that best betokened God's presence. For in its journey across the universe to touch and penetrate me, it had traversed the same course as God traversed when he sought me to speak to me.

It has never been an effort for me to think of creatures, all creatures, as messengers of God, as his signs.

I never wearied of repeating to my companions that creatures *were tokens of God.*

In fact, this is the way I began to pray:

> *All praise be yours, my Lord,*
> *through all that you have made,*
> *And first my lord, Brother Sun,*
> *who brings the day;*
> *and light you give to us through him.*

How beautiful he is, how radiant in all his splendor.
Of you, Most High, he bears the likeness.

Yes, he bears a token.

Creatures are God's "tokens."

They contain his presence.

They contain it, they live it, they express it with crystal chastity, without possessing it utterly.

These "things," creatures, have the ability to lead us little by little to that species of contemplation which, as it requires our commitment as well, is known as "acquired" contemplation, and it is the fountain of great joy. I would look at the sun and give it a smile.

Then I would say, "I love you."

Of course I noticed I had not said "I love you" to the sun itself, but to the one it betokened—God, of whom the sun is a sign.

This conversation with creatures was something extraordinary, and it gave joy to my very body, so that I felt like leaping, shouting, singing.

I felt myself to be steeped in God, as I was steeped in everything I touched and everything I saw.

Everything was one, and to deny God would have been tantamount to denying creatures, denying the light, denying the real.

Thus there was no denying God, no, not even if all things had returned within the mystery of that Personhood of his that transcended forever the universe that contained them.

"Mystery"—which had disturbed me for a time—now revealed itself to me, gradually, as one of the most interesting and extraordinary elements of creation.

Mystery was a space spread out around me by God out of respect for my littleness and my liberty.

It was the gentle shadow of that sublime alcove where All and Nothing meet to embrace, and forever to deepen their knowledge of each other, and to unveil themselves to each other without violence and without burning their eyes with too much light.

The wind was the sign of things' motility, of their inexhaustible thrust to go forth and seek. It was the voice of the lover, arriving unexpectedly. It was the experience of him who had succeeded in tearing me out of my solitude. It was the caress that was always there. It was inexhaustible, a continuously intensifying impact.

Pentecost itself had been betokened by a wind—coming like a hurricane and rattling all the doors.

I loved to say:

All praise be yours, my Lord, for Brothers Wind and Air.

Then what can I say of fire?

It poured forth speech in a torrent, and its words were never ended. There was nothing I could not see in it as I fixed it in my gaze in the dark of night—which, like the dark of faith, is the instant that precedes the radiant light.

Life, death, time, space, the infinite, earth, sky, love, health, sorrow, joy, an embrace, everything—everything could be betokened by fire, even the reason for life: the inexhaustible gift of self, the warmth that bursts forth from the slow consuming of the giver.

It was most sweet to me to pray, along with fire:

All praise be yours, my Lord, through Brother Fire,
through whom you brighten the night.
How beautiful he is, how gay! Full of power and strength.

❧

It did not take me much time to compose the Canticle of Creatures at Saint Damian.

When it seemed I had it ready, I called my companions and we sang it together.

I began truly to taste the joy of praying together.

And now I must tell you something personal.

Whenever I began to pray, I seemed to lift my arms spontaneously.

I felt myself to be at the center of the universe, where all things, flowers, birds, stars, seemed to crowd around to praise God with me.

I became creation's voice, the priest of all that was little and insignificant and without a voice.

This uplifted me. In this task I discovered my secret calling.

Few words in Scripture had struck me as had Peter's statement in his first Letter: "You are a priestly people."

I was soothed.

I had never desired to be ordained a priest, and my companions knew this very well.

I kept the true reasons to myself, with joy, for these matters are difficult to explain.

But the happier I was not to be a priest, the more I felt I was a priest.

It was like a late vocation, and I would have been happy if I could have shared it with my whole Order.

It seemed to me that priests—the ones ordained by the Bishop—were in the Church precisely for the purpose of saying to all men, absolutely all of them (and even more to all women, absolutely all of them): "You are all priests, for you belong to a priestly people."

So I was quite comfortable praying with arms extended, or when I blessed birds or fishes with my hand.

Yes, I was experiencing in life what you now sing so nicely (and I thank the author):

> *How sweet to feel*
> *in my heart*
> *now, humbly;*
> *love born.*

How sweet the understanding
that I am no longer alone,
but part
of an immense life,
generous and resplendent around me.

And now, brother or sister born nearly eight centuries after me, and one with me in faith in the same Lord God, let us continue to pray together.

Here is my prayer of those days, in the very words
    of those days.
Most high, all-powerful, all good. Lord!
All praise is yours, all glory, all honor
And all blessing.
To you, alone, Most High, do they belong.
No mortal lips are worthy
To pronounce your name.
All praise be yours, my Lord, through all that you have
    made,
And first my lord, Brother Sun,
Who brings the day; light you give us through him.
How beautiful is he, how radiant in all his splendor!
Of you, Most High, he bears the likeness.
All praise be yours, my Lord, through Sister Moon
    and Stars;
In the heavens you have made them, bright
And precious and fair.
All praise be yours, my Lord, through Brothers Wind
    and Air,
And fair and stormy, all the weather's moods,
By which you cherish all that you have made.
All praise be yours, my Lord, through Sister Water,
So useful, lowly; precious and pure.
All praise be yours, my Lord, through Brother Fire,

Through whom you brighten up the night.
How beautiful is he, how gay! Full of power
    and strength.
All praise be yours, my Lord, through Sister Earth, our
    mother,
Who feeds us in her sovereignty and produces
Various fruits with colored flowers and herbs.

Let us pause for now, and finish later—when you have learned to bear sorrow by loving.

For my story, too, is long. And before I could say, *"All praise be yours, my Lord, for Sister Death,"* I had to walk a while, and stay long and patiently at the school of Jesus' cross.

⚘

Still another fountain of gladness in me was the sense of liberation the Gospel gave me.

The feeling of having been freed from slavery was a constant cause of gladness.

I, Francis, had been liberated from the idols—from fear, from my complexes.

I felt happy. I made Psalm 114 mine, and I prayed in its words:

When Israel came out of Egypt,
the House of Jacob from a foreign nation,
Juda became his sanctuary;
Israel his domain.

It was as if I said,

When Francis left his house,
and began to reason, as a free human being,
God became his All,
and the things of God became his love.

The sea looked, and drew back in astonishment,
the Jordan turned about and flowed backward,
the mountains leapt like rams,
the hills leaped like lambs of my flock.
What has come over you, sea, that you run away;
and you, Jordan, that you go the other way?
Why do you mountains leap up like rams
and you hills like lambs of my flock?

What a wonderful thing.

Even nature shared our joy.

It was a grand thing to see a human being break free of slavery so that even the seas and the mountains took part in the feast and the dancing.

Are you astonished if the wood of Saint Mary of the Angels seemed to catch fire at night when we were praying?

Does it seem strange to you that roses might bloom in winter?

And that wolves would grow tame?

And that fish would listen to us?

No, brothers and sisters, rather be surprised if the opposite occurs, be astonished if you see a sky that does not move with distraction at your joy.

All is one, and everything partakes of the same feast.

You have only to see.

❧

But to see, you have to look well.

I have already told you that before my conversion, I had not seen creatures.

They had passed me by as if they were something foreign, like landscapes.

Now I saw them.

And I fixed them well with my regard. I noticed that they looked very hard at me, too.

Perhaps—why not?—they sought to communicate, even as I.
Perhaps, I thought, they would understand me.

So I made an effort to speak with them, and I succeeded.

One day I was crossing Lake Rieti, rowing toward the
hermitage of Greccio, when a fisherman honored me with a
live water fowl.

I accepted it with pleasure, then opened my hand so that
he could fly away.

But the little bird refused to do so, settling down into my
hand as if he were on a nest.

Then, as it happened, I began to pray, and took leave of
my senses. Coming to myself afterward, as if returning from
a long journey, I was surprised to see the same bird once
more, looking at me with his little head cocked to the left.

I gazed upon him with love and bade him depart. But he
awaited my benediction.

Then he flew sweetly away.

And I wonder what I ought to tell you about the friendship there was between me and a falcon.

Well, I was in a certain hermitage, where I had withdrawn
to pray in peace.

I noticed that very nearby there was a falcon, with its nest.

We became friends. We took our meals together and
peered at each other from a distance.

Then the falcon undertook to rouse me from my rest
at the hour of prayer—at midnight, and again at dawn for
Lauds. And he did this regularly.

He always performed his duty with precision.

Once he even went beyond the call of duty.

He had noticed that I was not feeling well—and so he did
not awaken me in the night, but only in the morning for
Lauds.

I think God was guiding me by the falcon.

You can go ahead and smile. And you are right to smile,
because you have never had this experience. But it happened

to me, and I took pleasure in it all, even going so far as to hold conversations with all manner of creatures, and preach various sermons to them.

Nature, animals—they are so accustomed to seeing the enemy in human beings that they scamper away at our very approach.

Generation upon generation of human beings have done nothing but beat, kill, and torture animals.

And the animals have inherited a fear complex for human beings, so that now they either menace us, or run away in terror.

I made an effort to make them understand that I was a friend. At first they were astounded and incredulous. But then they believed.

And they drew near.

And they listened to me.

I can tell you, there was so much happiness in my body that I was no longer in the flesh.

It was as if the dimensions of the Kingdom had been enlarged for me.

It was as if I had been given new proofs for the existence of God.

It was as if the number of my sisters and brothers had become measurelessly greater.

One day at the Portiuncula, on a fig tree near my cell, I spied a cicada singing at the top of her lungs.

I stretched out my hand toward her and called, "My sister Cicada, come to me!" And she came, as if she had understood me, and there she was, on my hand. So I told her, "Sing, my sister Cicada, and joyfully praise the Lord, your creator and mine!"

She obeyed without a moment's hesitation.

Yes, she began to sing, and did not leave off until I too had begun to praise the Lord in song. When she heard me she fell silent. Then, when I paused, she took up the chant, just as if we were singing in antiphonal choir.

She stayed with me for a week, living on a limb at the door of my cell. Whenever I passed by I would caress her, and she submitted to my hand as if she enjoyed it.

And no sooner had I said to her, "Sister Cicada, sing!" than she would fill my cell with her song.

Once near Greccio, a confrere brought a rabbit to me.

He had caught it in a snare.

I spoke to the little beast. "Brother Rabbit, how did you get yourself snared? Come here to me."

And the little animal, free now, suddenly leapt up to my lap and grew calm, nestling tamely in my lap.

After a bit I lovingly caressed him and told him, "Now go, return to your freedom in the wood." And I placed him gently on the ground. But he turned and leapt back at once into my arms!

He stayed with me and would not leave me. Finally I bade the friars, "Bear him to the wood." After that I saw him no longer.

Yes, you can smile!

You are too rationalistic, you modern people, and this is one of the reasons why you are so sorrowful.

I have experienced the unity that obtains between nature and its crown. And I have understood that often, even though that oneness is all around us, we fail to perceive it.

We are blind, and most things escape us.

I think only children generally understand such things. We may not take much account of children, but it is they who see best.

It was with good reason that Jesus said, "If you will not be children . . . you shall not enter."

I liked children, and I liked grown-ups with the heart of a child even more.

What a marvel!

What a joy, to be with them!

To be with the like of Brother Juniper.

I remember it well.

One day, Brother Juniper had received a stiff dressing-down from the superior for having given away some silver bells which adorned the altar, without having received permission to do so.

And Brother Juniper thought to himself, "My, how the Guardian shouted just now. I'll wager he weakened his voice."

So he went to the kitchen and made some butter porridge.

Then in the middle of the night he went tap-tap-tapping at the general's cell, and when the general opened up there was Brother Juniper, candle in one hand and a bowl of hot porridge in the other.

"What is the meaning of this?" demanded the Friar Guardian.

And Brother Juniper: "Well, Father, today when you shouted at me for my faults, I could hear your voice getting feeble—getting too tired, I guess—so I thought I'd make you this porridge. It will moisturize your chest and throat."

At a brand-new scolding from the superior, who told him to go to the devil for arousing him, Brother Juniper responded, "That's all right, Father—then you hold the candle and I'll eat the porridge."

Yes, how much joy I have had from the brothers who were the most simple, the most transparent. I would have wished the whole congregation to be like them, for I understood that to overcome Satan and the world it was they who were the best soldiers.

The too intelligent frightened me.

I felt that the complex reality of the universe was something to be faced with humor.

It was the best way to stand firm in the fray.

When, for example, I beheld Fra Rufinus, one of the illustrious men of Assisi, preaching in nothing but his underwear before the smiles of the pious ladies—well, I felt then that it was only with people of this mold that the world could be changed.

And when I saw Fra Bernard da Quintavalle appearing before me after the alms-collection empty-handed, half starved, and excusing himself for having eaten some crumbs along the way as if this had been a fault, I wept for joy, and felt I was truly the brother of all men and women.

That was gladness.

My Church, My Church

But it was not only the little church of Saint Mary of the Angels, and the woods surrounding it that was our refuge, our peace, and the place of our prayer.

It was the great Church as well, the one that reached from one end of the earth to the other, the one founded by Jesus himself—who at Saint Damian had spoken to me, telling me straight out, "Repair it."

At once I had set about attempting to repair the crumbling walls of Saint Damian. But I quickly realized that the Lord's words must have meant something much more vast. They must have had to do with the Church of Rome.

Where would we have been without this Church?

Who would have handed down to us, across twenty centuries, the teachings of our dear Lord Jesus?

Who would have encouraged us in the truth, reassured us in the path we had undertaken?

I, Francis, felt the need to lean on someone, to be reassured by someone.

It frightened me to bear responsibility alone.

So why not go to Rome and see the Pope?

Tell him the whole story—tell him of our desire to live the Gospel, nothing but the Gospel—and beg his blessing.

Confide to him our thirst for poverty, our dream of being with the poor, of putting ourselves in last place, of accepting the juridical status of the pauper, of the exploited, of the starving, of the homeless, of the nomad!

Presumption?

Were we asking the impossible?

How few we were! There were but a dozen of us then. And we already felt the need of recounting our affairs to the Vicar of Christ?

Was this not contrary to the humility we sought to live?

No, it was not, and we all set out together for Rome.

It was May, 1210.

I, Francis, carried a simple rule with me, drawn directly from the words of the Gospel, which seemed to me to express very well our common desire to consecrate ourselves to God in poverty and love.

All along the way, our singing and praying never stopped.

What joy we had within! And our joy spread among the people we met like an epidemic.

Food and lodging were no problem, even though the regions we were passing through were poor.

Everyone crowded around with curiosity, and when evening came there were always far more offers of lodging than we could use.

In Rome we went to see our own bishop, Guido. And it was very nice to hear him tell us right out not to look elsewhere, but simply to continue to lead our life in his diocese, for he was happy with us. He even promised to present us to the Pope, for he was friends with Cardinal John Colonna di San Paolo.

Innocent III, a true prince by blood, was a pessimist when it came to humankind. He lived in the sorrow of battle. Battles raged all around him, especially with the Albigenses, who preached poverty but spoke ill of the Church of Rome.

I had a vague notion that there would be a struggle. I was

insisting upon rigorous poverty, and the winds of protest and rebellion that agitated the Church were certainly not going to help me.

But what else could I do?

Was I to repudiate my spouse, my Lady Poverty, for the satisfaction of an approbation based on human prudence and common sense?

No, I thought not.

And then I had these eleven scarecrows standing around me. One look from them and I would have been contradicted.

But we were poor, very poor, and our poverty was like a slap in the face to the men who now surrounded us.

The Pope regarded me intently, and I looked at him with love.

"Little children, your life appears to us to be too harsh. We have no doubt that you, who have such fervor, are able to endure it; but We fear for those who will come after you."

"My Lord Pope, I give myself entirely to my Lord Jesus Christ. How can he fail in the promises he has made to those who abandon all for him?"

And we withdrew.

We spent our time of waiting in caring for the sick in the Hospital of Saint Anthony. The Pope spent it discussing our affair with the cardinals.

We knew that many cardinals were against our proposition, and had cast a negative vote.

We also knew that Cardinal Colonna was defending us, with a thesis very simple and concrete: *"If we refuse this little poor person's request, based as it is upon the Gospel—will we not displease God? And if we adopt the position that this rule of his is beyond human capacity; will this not be tantamount to admitting that men and women are incapable of following the Gospel on this earth?"*

The Pope sent for us, and once more we found ourselves in the great hall in his presence.

On high, Innocent III, pale, as if he had not slept the night. And before him, I, Francis, surrounded by my disheveled company.

The Pontiff fixed me with his eyes. He seemed to wish to plumb the depths of me, as I stood there before him.

I sought to defend my dream of living poverty in the Church by means of a parable, which I had first recounted to my companions.

I waxed eloquent, I employed all the strength at my disposal to say that we ought to be poor, and that this was a witness we could bear, to the benefit of the Christian people.

I do not know what happened at that instant.

It was as if the Pope suddenly changed his mind, as if a vexing problem had been resolved for him, all at once.

He smiled. He motioned me to approach, and embraced me. I understood that the battle was won, that God had intervened to assure the Pope we were serious, and had no wish to deceive the Church.

Later it was reported that the Pontiff had had a dream.

It was whispered that he had seen the Church of Saint John Lateran about to collapse—and a person dressed like a poor man supporting it with his shoulders.

Was I that poor person?

It took courage to think so.

And then dreams—how can you believe in dreams?

And so whenever that thought returned to my mind I sought to chase it away, telling my Lord of all my nothingness, and protesting my lack of ability.

And now we were on the road again, with Rome at our backs.

❧

Our first great elation, at the approval bestowed by the Pope on our rule, soon gave way to a certain vague uneasiness.

As we neared Umbria our songs grew fewer and were replaced by the silent prayer that welled up within us. For we were seized with an awareness of the difficulties we were approaching.

One thing was sure, and we could count on it: God was with us, and would be helping us, but the real battle lay before us.

We had seen no poverty in the halls of the Vatican. We had found no signs to indicate there was any there.

This, I felt, would provoke discussions among the little company presently toddling along toward Assisi, all enthusiastic to live the poverty of the Gospel, but at the same time made up of simple, unsophisticated, ungainly folk.

I could not sleep at night.

In the situation in which we found ourselves was the whole mystery of the holy and sinful Church, at once indefectible by divine promise, and capable of scandalizing. And indeed it did scandalize, by its riches and its might.

How could I solve this problem?

How could I speak with the brothers?

I felt, to the bottom of my being, the loyalty I wished to bear the Church, my mother, who had given me birth, who was my all; and at the same time I felt the contradiction of a shameless wealth, of an involvement with power politics, which weakened the message—and which God had even called to the notice of the Pope in his vision of the Lateran about to tumble down while the poor shoulders of the poor held back the crumbling walls.

We had to bolster the Church, keep it from crumbling. But how?

We had to repair the breaches. But which?

Suddenly I perceived a danger we could be risking, young and inexperienced as we were—that of turning into a band of malcontents, nervous and sour, judgmental, and quick to point the accusing finger at the festering sores of others.

No, that was no way. We would not have accomplished a thing.

There were too many preachers around like that already, especially in the North.

Jesus surely waited for something different from us.

And all of a sudden there it was. We were to imitate Jesus—to do as he had done. We turned his words over in our minds, and how sweetly.

"Judge not."

"Why do you stare at the speck of dust in your brother's or sister's eye and fail to see the timber in your own?"

"I have come not to judge but to save."

It was especially these last words that struck me, and pierced my innards.

"I have come to save."

Had I not been saved? And this was why I was so happy—because I had been saved.

And now who was I, who had been saved, to criticize those who had not had the same grace?

If anything I ought to have compassion.

The thought totally opened my eyes. It clarified the attitude I ought to have toward the rich, toward those who had not yet entered into the blessedness preached by Jesus.

The sinner, the rich man or woman with all the brocade, was poor, poorer than those who were visibly poor because they wore rags.

And if I had compassion for the visible poor and loved them, then why should I not have compassion for, why should I not love, these invisible rag-tags—the rich, the mighty, those who yet believe in idols and dwell in the dark?

Yes, I felt it, and with a jar: the unlucky ones who have not yet entered into the blessedness of the Gospel, the joy of liberation, and are still satiating themselves with vanity, anxiety, pride, avarice, and power.

Of my father and myself—which had been the lucky one?

I, singing free as a skylark and feeling God to be so very near—or he, who continued to be concerned with his money and his nonsense?

Of two persons of the Church, who was the more fortunate—the one who believed in the Gospel of Jesus, or the one who still believed in the violence of the Old Testament, dreaming only of heads to split for the glory of God? Yes, the Gospel had indeed been proclaimed, but one who did not live it was a good deal more unhappy and unlucky than one who had been penetrated by it.

Between Zacchaeus, entering into the mind of Jesus and becoming poor, and the rich man, parting company with Christ out of fear of poverty, and remaining in slavery— whom ought I consider the happier?

Now I had understood. I had found the approach to use in speaking to my companions in faith.

"Brothers and sisters, we are juniors—the lowest, the least. Minors, if you will. And we should remain minors. The place for us is the one Jesus chose: the last."

But precisely because the last place is the loveliest.

If we take the last place no one will envy us, no one will be scandalized at us, no one will fear us.

We shall be able to see things better from there, from the last place; we shall be able more easily to understand those who suffer, those for whom we wish to toil.

The only thing we have to fear is pride, the wish for advancement, and the wish to judge our brothers and sisters— to strike down with our judgments those who are already bitterly struck down by the absence of God and the sorrow sin leaves behind.

Our true rule is the Gospel, and we should consider blessed those who have understood, and who live poverty, chastity, meekness, peace, and persecutions, as their beatitudes.

If anyone deserves compassion it is the rich person, the powerful person, the satisfied person, upon whom there weighs the terrible word of God, "Alas for you!"

⸎

The Fourth Beatitude in the Gospel of Matthew, *"Blessed are the merciful,"* was now the light of my path.

Mercy for sinners.

Mercy for Christians.

Mercy for the Church.

Mercy for Popes.

Mercy for our own selves, who had the desire to be poor, but who did not succeed.

Yes, even the Church had need of the glance of mercy. Even the Vatican.

Until now, I had not well understood in what the mystery of the Church consisted: sinfulness, and infallibility; bad example, and assurance along the road; fearful blindness in the shepherds, and the certainty of reaching the Land of Promise with precisely these shepherds.

Now I saw, and I was glad to have been in Rome and to have had Rome's approval.

I felt at peace.

I felt myself to be on solid rock.

I felt myself to be within God's design.

That God of Abraham, Isaac, and Jacob, who had struck an alliance with humanity.

That God of Moses, who had led his people from slavery to the Land of Promise.

That God of David, who in spite of the enormous sins of all his house had said to him: "Upon thy throne I shall place a king" who would never fail (cf. 1 Chron. 7:14).

That God of Israel, who makes a divine promise to live by: *"Fear not, I shall be with you. I will lead you. You will conquer!"*

The infallibility of Christ did not rest on the weakness of human beings, but on the divine omnipotence.

It was not the result of human virtue, but of the love of God, which, in spite of human beings' little virtue and their infantile mistakes, will succeed, with his invincible will, in leading his people to their goal.

In establishing Moses, Saint Peter, and Innocent III as heads of his people, God did not remove from them their hardness of mind or the dross of their heart—but in spite of the hardness and the dross he guaranteed his people that they would reach the Kingdom.

It was not a matter of switching leaders, then, and founding another Church. It was a matter of believing that the Church had already been founded, and that we should trust in the Spirit that guided it as he had guided Moses, as he had guided David, as he had guided Peter, and as he now guided Innocent III, whom we had seen in all his weakness but a few days before.

Yes, what was needed was to believe that the Church had already been founded before we appeared on the scene, and that we would not have been better than the others.

Perish the thought that we would have been more skillful because we were ill clad and lived in huts!

Perish the temptation that once we had come on the scene things would have taken a sharp turn for the better!

No.

We, as Church, would have continued to be saints and sinners, capable of high ideals and base enormities, the dwelling place of peace and a jungle of violence.

All would have depended upon personal sanctity—on the commitment and the prayer of saints, on the sacrifice of the humble, on the true love of Christ's followers.

But one thing was sure: even if we had failed, overwhelmed by our sins and our faithlessness, the Church would not have failed—as neither did God's people fail in the desert, or in the terrible loneliness of Babylon.

The "little remnant" would have arrived nonetheless.

God himself was the guarantor.

☙

My Church, my church,
homely as you are
you are ever my Church!

This is what I would sing, to my guitar, were I to come one night to Assisi to see how things were coming on.

And I would mean it for the great Church as well as for the little church that is mine, the Franciscan one there.

You see, I would invite the sleepy friars who came to meet me, to see their Francis once again, "Let us go up to the Rock and talk a while."

The moon is bright tonight. Of course, no one notices the moon any longer, for the commune has illuminated your houses with an artificial lighting arrangement that is truly wonderful. I have to admit that your houses are very beautiful, and that the floodlights show them nicely. It is a pleasure to behold them.

While I was alive I never would have thought that you might transform Assisi into such a gracious little city, so full of harmony.

What marvels these basilicas are! Good job, Friars!

I, Francis, admire the unity, the gentle loveliness, in the architecture of your houses.

Oh, it would be easy to reproach you for certain things which are not exactly to my taste, but I shall not.

I, too, have matured over the years, and I would no longer raze religious houses to the ground as I did in those days.

Eight centuries have gone by, and poverty can have different expressions. I was a dreamer—such a dreamer that I was abruptly replaced by a nondreamer, Fra Elias.

Yes, you can reproach me, I do not mind. But I ask you not to overdo. A certain spreader of ill rumors, a Franciscan Tertiary who works in a bank, mentioned to me that your accounts there are rather considerable.

And I intend to go into the matter—even though I shall also have to reproach my Tertiary for violating banker's confidentiality.

But I do ask you one thing.

If you do have money, spend it well. Spend it on the poor, whom we have loved so much, you and I.

If I come to Assisi during the centenary dressed as a pilgrim—and I shall—do not tell me you have no room and shut the door in my face.

Lodge me, as someone poor. Give me work to do, but lodge me.

How ironic and deformed, that you, of all people, should shut the door in the face of the poor who cannot pay.

Do you not agree?

And something else.

If you lodge me, allow me to pray with you. In the morning and in the evening.

In the morning we can pray Lauds together. And I shall congratulate myself if we can do this without having to hear, "This fresco, ladies and gentlemen, dates from the fifteenth century."

And in the evening, if we assemble with the tourists to pray, and sing Vespers together, I beg you, see that silence is observed.

This is important, and there are people who like it.

You see, if people do not find a mature spiritual atmosphere, after they have left they speak ill of you, and say that you have transformed the church into a museum, and that you like to strut about playing tourist guide.

This is not well. Do you not agree?

But why are you staring at me? Are you not happy with what I have said?

Do you want a sterner sermon?

I gave you one—eight hundred years ago. This time I shall content myself with less.

And then I too have learned something, in all these centuries, and I would like to tell you what it is.

Judgments on the question of poverty are difficult to make.

The garb of a pauper, a small house, a wooden table, a chipped cup, the plaited haversack—these are external signs. Then there is the reality, the true poverty, which is altogether interior and invisible.

Today, I prefer the reality. And I actually see it is better, see it in its real essence, because now it has become something more vast, and universal.

The one who cannot meet the rent is not the only poor person. He or she is poor as well who is suffering from cancer.

Those who live in burned-out slums are not the only poor. He or she is poor as well who is on drugs, who is unloved, who is marginalized, who is alone.

And then there is something else not very much to my liking—something which we would not have dreamed of doing in my time, yet you do it.

In poverty, you have begun to cheat at the game.

You see, it has become fashionable for young people to dress badly. They put on work clothes even if they are going to a party.

And there are those who actually prefer old cups and old tables. These are now known as "antiques," rarities.

So it is difficult to judge.

And I do not wish to judge.

So I only say, place yourselves directly before God and be judged by him.

And keep one thing in mind.

At the vespers of your life you will be judged by your love, not by your poverty.

I say this because out on the frontiers of the Church poverty has become a battlefield, where the poor hate the rich, and the laborer hates his or her employer.

This is no longer blessedness. It is not even Gospel. This is Marxism.

Have you still failed to notice how easily one inhales the spirit of the times? And the spirit of the times is not the spirit of the Gospel.

There is no longer any appreciable difference between a union organizer who is Christian and one who is of another culture altogether.

This is sad, very sad. Is prophecy dead?

Never forget, God is love. Poverty is but his garment.

Then do not seek poverty unless you are still capable of seeing, supporting, and loving the person who wears it,

even if that person is a sinner,

even if that person is a member of the middle or upper class,

even if that person is, may I say, a bishop or monsignor.

&

Still another thing occurs to me. Please excuse me if I insist on it.

You are living in a strange day—a contradictory one, an ambiguous one.

You have more wealth than before, and you talk more of poverty. You are middle class and you play "poor Church." You talk more of community, and you live more isolated, more divorced, from one another.

"Many a slip 'twixt the cup and the lip," they say—and there is a whole ocean of slips between what you say and what you do.

It is the ocean of your chatter, and you are drowning in it in every regard.

Now would you care to know why I am not inclined to give you a "tough talking-to"? Because you are the tough ones, not I.

All one has to do is to listen to you when you gather together.

It is a terrible thing, how hard, unyielding, and radical you are.

What a pity that this hardness, this radicalism, is always directed against others and never against yourselves.

One would say that your great passion is to convert others!

And I, Francis, tell you, aim at your own conversion. You will see that you will understand things better.

Above all, understand this: it is of no use to think you can change the Franciscans, the Capuchins, the Conventuals, and to continue, the Jesuits, the Salesians, the Little Brothers.

It is simply not possible!

What is possible is the conversion of a person—especially if that person happens to be you who are listening to me at this moment.

History has its own laws, and no institution escapes the ravages of time, however holy and great its founder.

Only naked human beings, as naked as possible, can escape the ravages of time, and are able to place themselves before the nakedness of the Gospel and make it their own.

My children—this is what I shall call you, since you call me Father Francis—do not believe in the reform of your Order. Believe in your personal reform.

My brothers and sisters—for you call me Friar Francis—be holy, and the world will appear to you as holy.

The Eloquence of Signs

One thing I grasped very soon after my conversion to the Gospel. It was the power of signs.

I had joyfully perceived that all around me was a sign of God, his token, and I no longer managed to look at anything without thinking of him, my Most High and Good Lord.

I can say that I felt immersed in him day and night, and no power on earth could distract me from that Presence, so sweet, so strong, so real. It was in this school that I learned to understand and live something very important, a fundamental lesson.

And it was this. As God bestowed upon us signs of himself, in order to speak to us, to explain things, so we too ought to do as much—both lest we lose time, and in order to check up on ourselves along our path and correct our weaknesses.

Yes, posit signs, leave signs. A concrete unfurling of our thought, the witness of what we wished to be: catechists of the Gospel lived.

I recall one of the first signs that occurred to my mind. This, I felt, would clearly indicate a scorn of money and victory over greed.

Bernard da Quintavalle and Peter Cattani had come to

join me, had asked to be my companions. Now, Bernard was very wealthy, and Peter was a priest and monsignor.

"Open the Gospel at random," I said to them, "and read whatever your eyes fall upon."

And what they read was, "If you wish to be perfect, go, sell what you have, give it to the poor, then come follow me."

Brothers, have you understood what the Lord wishes?

Yes.

They went. Bernard sold his possessions and Peter renounced his prelacy.

I can still see that May morning in the year 1208, in Saint Peter's Square in Assisi.

Bernard had a whole barrelful of things. I took some money and began to distribute it.

What a hullaballoo that morning!

People were appearing from everywhere and nowhere. There were the poor, and there were the not so poor. Everyone was clutching at everything he or she could lay hands on.

And we gave out everything, every last cent.

What joy of liberation I felt that morning! And I saw, in that sign, all humanity's slavery to money.

Another sign which I sought, with simplicity, to bestow upon my brothers and myself, was when I had asked Fra Rufinus to go and preach in Assisi.

Listen to what happened, in the lovely language of the Little Flowers of Saint Francis. Rufinus replied:

"Reverend Father, I pray thee, pardon me and send me not, for as much as I, as you know, have not the grace of preaching, and am a simple person, indeed an idiot."

And Francis spoke.

"Since thou hast not promptly obeyed, now I enjoin thee by holy obedience to go to Assisi, naked as thou wast born, in nothing but thy underclothing, enter a church, and preach to the people naked."

At this command, the said Fra Rufinus did divest himself and did come to Assisi, and did enter into a church, and having made a reverence to the altar, did ascend the pulpit and commence to preach.

At this the lads and men commenced to laugh, saying, "Now see we that those who practice such penances grow foolish, and take leave of their senses."

In this way Saint Francis, thinking once more upon the prompt obedience of Fra Rufinus, who was one of the most noble men of Assisi, and of the hard command which he had imposed upon him, commenced to catch himself up, saying, "Whence unto thee such presumption, son of Pietro da Bernardone, worthless little man that thou art, to enjoin Fra Rufinus to go preach the Gospel to the people naked like a madman? By God, do thou now prove in thyself what thou enjoinest others."

And of a sudden in the fervor of the spirit he divested himself, and went off to Assisi naked to preach.

I need not relate the rest, for you know what happened. But I wager Rufinus and I were long remembered for those sermons.

I often meditated on confidence in God at that time, on the simplicity which we ought to have toward him, and on our certitude of being guided by him and being borne like little children in his arms.

Listen to this sign.

Saint Francis was walking along a road one day with Fra Masseo. Now, the said Fra Masseo was somewhat in advance of the other. Arriving at a crossroads, at which one could turn toward Florence or Siena or Arezzo, Fra Masseo spoke, and said:

"Father, by which route should we proceed?"

And Saint Francis replied, "By that one which God will show us."

And Fra Masseo: "But how shall we know God's will?"

Saint Francis replied, "By the sign which I shall show thee. Whence I do enjoin thee, in virtue of holy obedience, that, at this crossroads, on that spot upon which thou now standest, thou turnest thyself round and round as children do, and leavest not off turning until I shall say thee."

And Fra Masseo commenced to turn about. And he turned so, that he fell many times upon the ground from the giddiness of his head; but as Saint Francis had told him not to leave off, and as he wished to be faithfully obedient, he rose ever again and again.

At last, as he was turning at great speed, Saint Francis said to him, "Now stand still and move not."

And he stood still. And Saint Francis asked him, "Which way is thy face turned?"

Fra Masseo: "To Siena."

Saint Francis: "This is the way by which God wills that we should go."

As he strode along, Fra Masseo marveled mightily at the work which Saint Francis had made him to perform, like a child; and he grumbled interiorly.

I, Francis, must say that Fra Masseo enjoyed ample opportunity afterward to understand that it was indeed God who had intervened in the choice we made by such strange means and with such a childlike spirit.

For at Siena, three rival factions were at one another's throats.

At our arrival they were willing to hear us, and we spoke with simplicity and ardor.

God did the rest, and there was peace in Siena that day.

❧

Another sign which, as it happened, I placed before my brothers—so that they would remember to treat all persons sweetly, even robbers—was at the cloister of Monte Casale, recently built, where I had installed as Guardian a dear little brother called Agnolo.

Now, there were three robbers roving the countryside. And one day they happened upon our house.

Fra Agnolo recognized them, and drove them away with expressions suited to the occasion.

At this point I, Francis, arrived with the alms I had been collecting, which included, besides bread, a fine jug of wine. I came to know of the manner in which Fra Agnolo had driven off the robbers.

I reproved him in order to help him remember that God can do all things, and that we are not called to judge, not even robbers.

"In view of the offense which thou hast committed against charity and against the sacred Gospel of Christ, I enjoin thee by holy obedience that thou forthwith take up this wallet of bread, which I have attached to this bottle of wine, and solicitously go after these robbers, over hill, over dale, until thou shalt have found them; and present them with this bread and with this wine on my behalf; and kneel before them and humbly declare thy cruel fault; and then beg them on my part to do no more evil but to fear God and offend not their neighbor; and if they do this, I promise to provide for their needs."

And while Fra Agnolo was on the way to do this command of Francis, the latter betook himself to prayer, and prayed God to soften the hearts of those robbers and to convert them to penitence.

And so it happened.

❧

Positing signs, leaving signs.

Setting up signs that speak, to call us back to truth and to love.

The entire liturgy is a living sign—a luminous call to things invisible.

When you light the Paschal candle, the sign of Christ died and risen, the assembly is drawn through that sign to the sweet memory of Jesus, who is consumed in giving us light. In the same way, in giving a sign of our scorn for money, we help our brothers and sisters understand their true liberation from the idols.

Just as, at Mass, you prostrate yourselves humbly before the Eucharistic Sign and renew the faith of all of you in the value of littleness before God—in the same way, that sign of the naked sermons, accepted with humility, recalled my brothers to the true sense of obedience.

Setting up signs.

In our days we suddenly set up a new sign: begging for alms.

I would have preferred to come right out and set up the sign of work as our form of the religious life. But this could not be done. Work, in my days, was a luxury—I mean paid labor, a job. Something like having a job in a bank would be for you today.

If we wished to reach the poor we had to accept the life of a beggar, and we accepted it to the hilt.

In setting up this sign we were telling the Church where the problem was; and to the beggars we were saying, "Courage! Here we are, in solidarity with you."

But today this token is out of place. No Friar of good sense should feel the need of looking for alms while the fields are short of hands. To beg one's bread as an alms when we can earn it with our work is nonsense, and can become a scandal.

Hence today, a fine sign of loving the poor would be work, especially if it is hard, dirty, ill-paid work.

What a pity that some ecclesiastics are still allergic to manual work performed by priests.

But they have plenty of excuse.

They come from a school of thought where work was considered incompatible with nobility and holiness. What can you do?

It is a last remnant of the past. The ancient Greeks scorned manual labor, and the middle class has never been enthusiastic about weariness and soiled clothes.

In my day a prelate would have been ashamed to carry a sack on his back down the street, or to work on a construction project.

What is astonishing is the ease with which the ecclesiastical world forgets the working-class origin of Christ and commits the absurdity of asserting that it is "not good" for priests to do "manual labor." This is a grave error, because it is the same as saying, "It is not good that Jesus is a carpenter!"

And I say this, I, Francis, without any ill will!

※

Another sign, set up by our houses, was the sign of asylum—of defense and aid for anyone who was suffering.

Just as a fugitive found refuge within a church, and no one would have dared strike him down there, so also the poor felt our houses to be places of refuge, where they could find bread, encouragement, and friendship.

This was our true glory, and I have to admit that the whole Church came to be signed by this boast.

And it still is today.

Every Christian house, every convent or monastery, every bishop's palace, had a door open to receive suffering humanity.

And these doors, if possible, while visible, were not too

frightening for the very poor—halls not too brilliant, stair-cases not too mammoth—which would have been a sign of might and grandeur rather than of humility and truth.

༄

In my rather childish enthusiasm I had often dreamed of selling off the Vatican and giving the proceeds to the poor. I dreamed of telling the Church that it was time to start being serious, to start matching the proclamation of the Word with deeds.

Now I, too, am grown up, and just as I no longer feel ill at ease when I see a big religious house, so too I can take a tour of the Vatican without going out of my mind.

But I am still just as convinced as I was eight centuries ago of the effectiveness of the signs which I set up in the sight of my brothers and sisters—and so I feel I ought to tell you one more thing.

And here, too, no polemics.

Imagine a group of pilgrims arriving in Rome, all joyful at the prospect of being able to pray in such beautiful basilicas, and of seeing the Pope and hearing his voice as if he were Jesus.

Well . . .

How do you think they would like to find,
along with the Gate of the Bells,
along with the Gate of Bronze,
along with the Gate of Saint Anne,
along with the entrance to the museum,
a little gate, bearing the inscription:
"Come to me, all you who labor and are overburdened, and I will give you rest" (Matt. 11:28)?

And to be able to go in and find a simple place, a poor place, but inviting and comfortable, where they would actu-ally meet a man or woman who would give them the sense of a Church alive and open to the poor?

Oh, it is not that charity is lacking in the Vatican, or in your works either.

I would put it this way. In all the great work of charity, what is often lacking is the sign.

Or if it is not actually lacking, it is often too big and showy, too efficient, and the poor are unable to grasp it, like an apostolic nunciature, a radio station, a cathedral, and a cardinal's apartment, all rolled into one.

Humanity today is sensitive to small signs—but concrete ones, intelligent ones, and especially signs that are the fruit of an act of love that is immediate and lived, with strength and constancy, right today.

Pope Wojtyla lifting a child in his arms above the heads of the crowd, prostrating himself to kiss the earth, weeping before a dolorous scene, entering an African hut or a South American pauper's dwelling—ah now, he sets up signs that speak all by themselves, and which place him in communion with the poor.

Is this not so?

And this is why I tell you that if I come to Rome, hidden in a group of pilgrims, I shall be looking at those famous walls to see whether there is a little door open in them that would fit me, Francis of Assisi.

The Primacy of Nonviolence

When I, Francis, happen to read the things which you have written of me since my death—so abundantly, and, I admit, in such good taste—I have to confess that what I like best is the account in the *Little Flowers.*

I feel comfortable there.

Sometimes it happens that I no longer recall whether the things recounted actually went that way, or instead are a bit exaggerated—or just plain made up?—but that has no importance.

I like them.

Even if they did not happen just that way, they are beautiful and good as told that way. I accept them all, for they give a photograph of me which, even if retouched by your generosity, is the photograph of nonviolence, a picture which I am honored to accept, and I thank you for having understood me.

For yes, that is what I was, nonviolent. And the Little Flowers are a beautiful dream for you and for me.

Deep within us, every one of us, are dreams of such a world, made peaceful with love and the sweetness of humility.

Is this not so?

Some of you may be inclined to smile at the episode of the wolf of Gubbio. But if you have ever been a child, truly a child, surely you too have desired to solve problems in this fashion, as I solved them at Gubbio that frosty morning in the new-fallen snow.

What deep symbols of humanity there are in that wolf fleeing human violence and finding himself in trouble from hunger!

I have to tell you, sisters and brothers, that I had pipe-dreamed of an incident like that years before, as a boy. I had been told that up there on the crests of the Apennines there were ravening wolves that came down to menace the flocks.

I did not know Christ then.

And yet I dreamed of going to find such a beast, armed only with caresses. And the beast would have halted before me.

And now that I knew the caresses of Jesus would I have been afraid?

Would I have armed myself with a pruning knife?

Would I have desired to see blood, even a wolf's blood, on the rocks of Gubbio?

No, brothers and sisters, I was not afraid.

Not since I had experienced the fact that my God is the God of the wolf, too.

What is extraordinary in the incident of the wolf of Gubbio is not that the wolf grew tame, but that the people of Gubbio grew tame—and that they ran to meet the cold and hungry wolf not with pruning knives and hatchets but with bread and hot porridge.

Here is the miracle of love: to discover that all creation is one, flung out into space by a God who is a Father, and that if you present yourself to it as he does—unarmed, and full of peace—creation will recognize you and meet you with a smile.

This is the principle of nonviolence, and I should like to

recommend it to you with all the enthusiasm of which I am capable.

I have asked you not to speak over much of poverty today. Your environment is too ambiguous in its regard, and it is too difficult to explain your position in your bourgeois and socialist milieu. Instead, I tell you this, and I tell you most emphatically: Speak of nonviolence, be apostles of nonviolence, become nonviolent.

Now is the hour to do so, in fact it may be the last hour, in as much as you are all sitting on top of a stockpile of bombs, and you can blow up at any moment now.

Do not underestimate the danger. I have a strong feeling that you will have to suffer a thing or two before the end of the world.

It would be better to be prepared. And it would be still better to hope for the conversion of humanity.

Even Nineveh was converted, and saved.

Listen.

Today, when you talk nonviolence, everyone understands what you are talking about. It is a discourse that is clear and simple, and with its dynamic you can change the face of the earth.

You speak a great deal about human rights today, and this is good.

Now, the first human right is not to be subjected to violence, to be left in peace.

This human right is one which is biblical in scope, and you should live it to the hilt.

But it is even broader than that. Much broader, in fact.

Nonviolence regards first of all nature, the skies, the seas, the mines, the forests, the air, water, the home.

These are the first objects of nonviolence. It is a terrible sin you have committed all around you, and I do not know whether or not you can still be saved.

You have violated the forests, defiled the seas, plundered everything like a bunch of bandits.

Your contempt for nature knows no bounds.

If there were a court of the skies, or of the seas, or of mines, you would all of you (or almost all) be under sentence of death.

And perhaps there is such a court. An invisible one. For your punishment has certainly begun.

You can scarcely breathe your air. Your food has become unhealthy. Cancer assaults you with more and more regularity.

And now that you have destroyed nearly everything you have appointed me patron saint of ecology. You have to admit it is a little late.

I do not know what I shall be able to do.

The pity is that it is always the same ones who govern: the powerful, the rich, the professional politicians.

Try the little ones in the government—the simple, the poets!

But who believes poets?

Try being governed by those who can still look at the stars at night, or spend an hour watching a beetle under a dry leaf in the forest, or dream over a glow-worm in a field of May wheat.

These are the ones who would see humanity's problems better. At least they would not commit such horrors.

You have reached the point of no return. And you have no reason to complain: it is you who have been irresponsible.

You continue to manufacture machinery that exhausts your raw material, and huge amounts of capital; and yet you do not offer the slightest assistance to the people who work the farms, where the world's real wealth is, and which are going to rack and ruin.

You turn out graduates only to enroll them in the ranks of the unemployed, and they become weary and mistrustful in your cities. You fail to seek to form young people who love constructive, simple toil, the toil of the artisan or of the farmer, young people who care more for a well-turned object or a loaf of whole-grain bread than they do for money.

※

If you need proof that you are off on the wrong track, consider well your sorrow.

It will tell you the size of your errors.

You are terribly sorrowful.

Gladness is a stranger to your homes—those excellently constructed homes of yours, where there is no humanity, and especially no humor.

But you have worked so hard! Do you not deserve at least a little tranquility after the effort you have expended?

The sad part is, you measure everything by money, and this is a mistake.

Laissez-faire capitalism, which has selected money as the driving force of its activity, is dying in its disasters and in its shames.

Marxism seemed to have found a better way. In place of money, Marxism put labor. But it, too, has almost totally failed to understand the human being.

It, too, has used human beings with violence, and has created systems just as depressing and pernicious as those it sought to replace.

It is not much fun to tour a socialist city!

Just as it is not easy to breathe in certain areas of New York or Tokyo.

At least you ought to admit that you have been wrong, and that you continue to be wrong, that you are bunglers. And what is worse, that you prostitute yourselves for money.

Is this not so?

Your basic mistake is that you place money instead of truth and love at the top of your scale of values.

After all, it is for money that you plunder nature, without the slightest thought that your errors will fall back upon your heads—as they are already doing.

But once done, a bad deed cannot be undone.

It would be more practical to cast a forward glance—knowing, however, that the conversion of human beings is not an easy matter.

Jeremiah said, "The heart of man is incurable."

In your position, not being an economist, perhaps I would follow the intuition of an amateur, without making five-year plans, and look only at the welfare of persons and of the world of nature.

I would start by giving the primacy to the countryside. I would consider cities the first mistake.

Why do the cities of Italy, of Brazil, and so on, present the horrible spectacle of human beings heaped up in matchbox suburbs and living in such inhuman fashion?

Because governments do nothing for rural areas, and the human beings who live there, afraid of being left helpless and abandoned, flee in the hope of bettering their situation.

If governments gave minimal aid to the people who live in the country, and sought to make their life a human one, most of them would stay to cultivate the land—which of course is ultimately what sustains all of you, even those of you who live in the city.

This recent era of your history has seen the exodus from the countryside. The era of nonviolence, of which I dream, should see an exodus from the cities, and a massive return to the country.

Country people ought to be helped to live even if they only keep the trees alive or clean the irrigation ditches. For they shall thereby be defending the land against destruction and neglect.

Make the land a garden, and the garden will become an Eden, and will give you what you seek: bread and peace.

If a youngster sells a motorbike to buy a bicycle, give him or her a reward. If a farm manages to get its electric power from a windmill, or by burning waste, see that this is given public praise.

If upstanding industrialists begin raising cattle, or sowing their estates with spices, tell them thanks and knight them!

And another thing.

Litterers should be arrested. And fine anyone cutting down a tree without absolute necessity.

A boy or girl who tramples a flower or torments a lizard should have to go to bed without any supper; and the politicians who destroyed the olive trees in the plain of Gioia Taura should be removed from office.

Ah, but I see I am only reciting more legends, à la the *Little Flowers*, and that some of you are beginning to smile again. You do not believe me.

Well, I am a dreamer.

I am Francis of Assisi.

❧

But to leave ecology for a moment, and turn to men and women—it is they, and they alone, who are responsible for the problem of violence. In fact they are the only creature in the universe that causes any problems at all.

Why are you so interested in the little story of the wolf of Gubbio?

Why have you filled it out with so many little details?

It interests you so very much—and yet it makes you smile. You do not really believe it.

In that little story you see the solution to the problems troubling you—yet at the same time you relegate it to the category of the utopias. A wolf tamed with a caress!

And yet, I have told you.

The miracle of that morning in Gubbio was not the conversion of the wolf, it was the conversion of the people who lived in Gubbio—who for a fleeting instant believed it was possible to overcome a wolf armed only with food to give him instead of weapons to bloody him.

Here you have the secret of everything.

Here is the absolutely basic secret, hidden in God's whole plan for humanity.

To believe in the possibility of the impossible.

To hope in things against all hope.

To love what does not seem lovable.

God's proposition to humanity is always wrapped in the veil of this mystery. And this is always the sum and substance of his request:

Can you believe?

Can you hope?

Can you love?

If you tell me yes, I shall give you the gift impossible.

Can you believe that God exists?

If you tell me yes, then God surely does exist—and you can sense his existence in your very faith.

Can you hope in eternal salvation?

Can you hope to be destined for a kingdom of truth, peace, and love?

If you tell me yes, then I shall make you smile with joy, and create a paradise in which to await you.

Can you love men and women as I loved them, placing myself at their service to the point of dying for them?

If you tell me yes, then I shall lead you to an experiential knowledge of myself, because it is love that will lead you to him who is love.

※

The Wolf of Gubbio is not a fairy tale to lull children to sleep. It is the most extraordinary truth, the one that could save the human race, especially today when it is sitting all together atop an immense stockpile of atom bombs.

Men and women all have the image of the wolf in other people.

If they allow themselves to succumb to this fear, and lose their calm, it is all over. There will be nothing left to do but shoot.

Hence your danger is not in the wickedness of the Americans or the Russians.

Your danger is in their fear of one another.

I know the Russians and the Americans well enough to think that they are not wicked enough to wish a holocaust.

But I know human nature well enough to know that if people are seized by fear they will try to press the button before the other can press it.

Now that human ingenuity has gotten people what they wanted, and technology has removed the limits in which they had found themselves—the truth has opened out like the blossom of an evil weed. The one, sole truth. Wickedness and violence are rooted in the fear of others.

If human beings go to war, it is because they fear someone.

Remove the fear, and you shall reestablish trust. And you shall have peace.

Nonviolence is fear's destruction.

This is why I tell you once more, I, Francis: Learn to conquer fear, as I did that morning when I went out to meet the wolf with a smile.

By conquering myself, I conquered the wolf.

By taming my wicked instincts, I tamed those of the wolf. By making an effort to trust the wolf, I found that the wolf trusted me.

My courage had established peace.

❧

You can deduce the rest by yourselves.

Just think what would happen one day if you became

nonviolent, and took the huge sums of money you spend to defend yourselves against fear and used it to help the people you fear.

When your young people, wasting away today in dejection, unemployment, and drugs, find their joy and their calling in the task of running hither and thither in the countries of the Third World, not only will you have solved the problems of others, you will have solved your own.

You will know peace then.

Is it too much to hope?

Perhaps someone is listening to me!

I, Francis, tell him or her: Courage.

The Dark Night

The more the years passed, the more I sought darkness and obscurity.

At first I attributed the phenomenon to a terrible pain in my eyes—due, the doctors told me, to diabetes. But eventually I grasped that there was something else invading my whole poor existence.

It was as if winter had penetrated me.

No longer did I thirst to see things. Even the sun no longer held its former fascination for me. Once it had betokened the Most High to me—thousands upon thousands of times. But now, when it arrived at my pupil it no longer spoke to me. I had the feeling that the sun was now within me, and had gone dark.

Now I nearly always prayed with my eyes closed; and I understand the friars more and more, especially the most mature of them, who sought out caves and grottos for their solitude, and the dark of night.

How many years the light had been for me the kindest companion when I wished to speak with God! But now it was darkness that attracted me, and its murky mysteriousness.

The word had yielded to silence, and it was silence that

returned upon me with the rhythm of things repeated, measured by my breath and the beating of my heart.

"*My God, my all,*" I repeated, again and again.

And that was really all I could say, for I was suffering very much.

There was good cause for my suffering. My company was going very ill.

My spiritual family was divided.

The knights of my Lady Poverty were unfaithful to their bride, more and more.

I felt unable to do anything for the brothers and sisters any longer. I felt that I had been wrong about everything—that time had smashed my dream.

Every day one friar or another would come to me to ask whether it would not be better to change the rule, or to tell me that what was needed was common sense.

I wanted huts, and the houses around me became more and more like fortresses.

I had so desired to live like the sparrows, without amassing anything. And now the pantries were getting bigger and bigger.

I had sought and loved companions like Juniper, Masseo, Leo, Egidio—true sheep of God, simple as water. And now, more and more, it was cultured and cunning men and women who entered our Order.

I could no longer bear it.

I went to seek comfort at Saint Damian, where Clare lived in perfect poverty; and I was helped by her counsel to stand firm in the struggle. But my strength was waning, and I felt swept away by events.

The cause of my suffering was the opinion, shared by those who seemed to be the most sensible persons of the Church, that it was impossible to live according to the rule of perfect poverty.

It was as if they were telling me that the Gospel could not

be lived on this earth in its integrity—*sineglossa*, as I had so often repeated to my brothers and sisters, without commentary, without glossing anything over.

To me, this sounded like treason toward Jesus—an act of doubting his word.

Once when Christmas was approaching, I wished to meditate once again on the life of Jesus as of someone poor, very poor. I set up a lifelike representation of the Cave of Bethlehem, at Greccia.

You see, I told everyone, you see? It is possible. Jesus himself lived in this way. God became poor, weak, little, and abandoned himself to the hand of history, trusting only in his Father.

You see, you see that it is possible—ever since God himself lived in this way!

But most people just savored a bit of sentimentality, and everything threatened to end in rhetoric.

Confronted with the facts of life, I heard myself saying: What is needed here is a little common sense. You see, Francis, one must put something aside for the winter. You see, Francis, the house has to have another wing; let us have a little prudence, after all. And then, we need books, many books.

The brothers and sisters ought to be educated persons.

It is not enough to read the Gospel!

And perhaps all this was true. But I could no longer bear it.

I had conceived and lived the word of Jesus in another fashion. I could not shake from my ears the refrain, "*Look at the birds in the sky.*"

This doubt in the ideal that had been my dream, this questioning of evangelical poverty, the sight of the friars becoming wise with the wisdom of this world—all this was unbearable to me, and I was consumed within.

The pain of seeing my life's most beautiful dream shattered was something far more cutting than the suffering caused by my diseased eyes.

&

Another source of pain for me was the mystery of a Church incredibly involved in political struggle.

To me, to be a Christian meant to be a witness of the tenderness of Jesus, a faithful follower of the lamb who went to slaughter without even bleating. And all around me, in the villages and cities where I went to announce the Word, all I saw were crosses on shields of steel, and swords, sharpened, as it was said, "for the defense of the Church."

Poor Church!

Poor Bride of Christ!

She herself, in full panoply, was preaching a crusade against the infidels, organizing alliances with the powerful, and involving herself in everything necessary for the victory.

Even the friars, my companions, whom I had so often told that our mission was to be meek and humble of heart, dreamed of crusades, and would not have hesitated to employ arms against the Muslims, on the excuse of giving glory to God by liberating the sepulcher of Christ.

Just where was it written in the Gospel that one had to liberate a tomb, even a tomb as illustrious as the tomb of Jesus?

Politics was everywhere now, and everything gave way before it as before a mighty, rushing torrent.

And my nonviolent ideal, my dream of going forth to meet human beings like lambs, was being shattered.

I had even managed, in the midst of such chaos, to make a voyage to Egypt, and actually to meet with Sultan Malek-el-kamel—if only to show myself and others that there was no need to be afraid to go out to meet the enemy unarmed. But my mission did not succeed.

The Sultan treated me well, and I returned home without

a scratch. But I did not care. I wanted peace. And instead
. . . I felt beaten, defeated, conquered.

℘

But where my cup of bitterness truly overflowed was at
the spectacle of the rifts that were forming in the Order—the
intestinal strife now raging between the innovators and those
who wished to remain strictly faithful to the rule.

The disputes on the rule paralyzed me. Unity was everything to me. Above all it was the sign of God's grace and
loving response to our efforts to be faithful to him.

The sight of the divisions among us, the sound of Gospel
texts being mouthed without meaning, and detached from
their original simplicity, destroyed me.

I really had the feeling that night had fallen upon what I
held most dear in the world—my family.

At the Pentecost Chapter, held in May of the year 1221,
the very triumph of our numbers increased my uneasiness.
We were more than five thousand.

I no longer felt capable of guiding the Order. Yet at the
same time I wanted to be in on everything.

Fortunately, I was thrust aside, and Fra Elias was elected
General.

Suddenly I felt comforted. I felt relieved of a responsibility
which had been weighing on me. But my peace did not last
long.

The most intransigent, those who claimed to be the most
loyal to me, turned to the assault, and the divisions became
more acute still.

Francis, you must come back. You must take up the reins
again. You must force your way back in.

Father, you must expel those who are the most dangerous.

And on the other hand, those who considered themselves
the pure ones, the spiritual ones, were growing eccentric,
unbalanced—on the excuse of fidelity to the original rule.

With their inhuman penances and repulsive appearance they actually drew reproval from the bishops.

No, I had certainly ruined everything.

It was night. The darkest night of my life.

Night without the presence of my God.

"My God, my God, why have you deserted me?" I repeated, again and again, like a lamentation.

Still, the official approval of the Church, which Pope Honorius had had the goodness to accord me with the Bull *Solet Annuere*, afforded me consolation.

I continued to go from house to house, but without finding any peace.

I would preach a little, then flee to a solitary hermitage—only to return at once to the street.

The place that held the most attraction for me in those years was Mount della Verna, where the friars had constructed a small house and had set up some peaceful little hermitages.

Mount della Verna was covered with woods. It had been given to us by Count Orlando, for prayer.

This was where I wished to spend Saint Michael's Fast, up there in one of those enormous clefts in the rock which had always enthralled me—and which were said to have been produced at the moment in Christ's Passion when the Gospel says the rocks split.

The thought of the Passion dominated me. I had the presentiment that I was about to fight life's last great battle and that I would find liberation only in identifying my sorrows with those of Jesus.

With me were Fra Leo, Fra Masseo, and Fra Angelo. Fra Masseo acted as our Guardian.

In their delicacy, and knowing my tastes, my loyal friends had reserved for me the place that would suit me best.

They had gone ahead and thrown a little bridge over a crevasse in the rock, by which I could easily reach the place they had selected for me—an extremely solitary and quiet one.

It was Fra Leo who had the task of coming to find me each day, carrying some bread and some water, and stopping at the bridge.

The password agreed on was from the Psalms: "Lord, open my lips" (Ps. 51:15). And if I responded by reciting the words that followed, that would be the sign that Fra Leo could cross over and enter my cell; otherwise he was to turn back.

❦

It was dawn, and the day was the fourteenth of September, the Feast of the Exaltation of the Holy Cross.

The night had been a terrible one, and my prayer had tasted bitter as death.

The temptation to leave the mountain and return to Assisi to take back the reins of government of the Order had been eating at me with continuous violence.

But now I had understood that I was to live, within myself, the very sacrifice of Abraham. *"Sacrifice your child,"* my conscience kept repeating—while the backlash of my wicked will impelled me once more to action instead.

Sacrifice your child!

Sacrifice what you hold dearest—your Order, your life's dream.

What saved me in that moment was the consideration of the Passion of Jesus.

How true it is that to solve our problems we must leave ourselves behind!

I cast myself forth from my self—and found myself to be on the way of Jesus' Calvary.

What was my sorrow when I looked at his?

What defeat mine, as compared with his?

And who was I, vile little man, obdurate sinner, before the majesty of the Son of God, before the holiness of the Word Incarnate?

Before him my poor scale of values was set on its ear, and my story became very small, my pains shrank away.

And his presence became gigantic.

His word became more strong.

And he spoke to me. "Francis, accept. As I accepted."

I accept, Lord!

Francis, sacrifice your life's work, as I sacrificed mine!

All betrayed me in my moment of trial.

I was left alone. More alone than you, who still have friends on this mountain.

Yes, I felt the need then to think of my own sorrows no longer, but to offer myself to be penetrated by, and to suffer with, those of Christ.

This prayer surged up within me with great force, and now I feel the desire to live it again:

> *Lord Jesus, two graces I ask of Thee before I die.*
>
> *First, to feel in my soul and in my body, as far as possible, the sorrow which Thou, sweet Jesus, didst endure in the hour of Thy most bitter passion; second, to feel in my heart, as far as possible, that extraordinary love with which Thou, O Son of God, wast inflamed, to the point of willingly undergoing so great a Passion for us sinners.*

Out beyond the confines of my self, by his pure gift of himself, I had entered into the life of the true mystery which ruled the invisible universe, and I had clutched, as only a poor person can, the revelation of true love.

What counted in life was not to do, but to love.

What saved the world was not our wisdom, and not our action: it was the power of the love of God, lived in each one of us.

On the human level, Christ's life was a failure. But on the level of his love, it was the masterpiece that gave new life to all creation.

By dying for love, Christ had exalted the whole world. Death had been vanquished.

❧

I closed my eyes, and let him do with me what he would. The silence was total. Even the birds kept still, though the dawn was bright and clear. Slowly, very slowly, I felt myself wrapped in a mysterious, radical embrace.

There came to my mind the words of Psalm 139: *"Lord, close behind and close in front you fence me round, shielding me with your hand."*

After a little while I was conscious of a very intense light before me, and I opened my eyes.

I saw a seraph, made of fire. He had six wings. And he was gazing at me more intently than anyone had ever looked at me in my life.

I had always thought of seraphim in this form, and I was happy that he was fixing me so with his gaze.

And when I had thought of what contemplation must be, as a revelation of God, I had thought of it as something like this.

Meanwhile something was being branded into my flesh. And I did not know *where,*
   or *how,*
   or *why are you doing this?*
But I knew it was Jesus.
And he united me to his passion.
And he revealed to me the secrets of God.
No, a truer revelation than this would never be.
If the world had been created, this was why.
If Jesus had redeemed us, this was why.
If the Father always pardoned us, this was why.

If the Church failed not on its march, this was why.

The embrace grew yet stronger upon me.

I felt a sharp pain, in my hands, in my feet, and even more in my heart.

I felt hot blood, too, running down my body.

I could bear the pain no longer—and yet I was buoyed up by a presence that made me happy.

I understood then that I had arrived at the mid-point of true happiness.

The solution for every anguish.

The open door of paradise.

❧

Whether or not I had the stigmata was a matter of no importance.

Whether or not I had open wounds, made by black nails, was of no consequence.

They would only have been signs, to be hidden as well as possible. What was of value is that the fire of the Holy Spirit had come within me, the same fire as had consecrated Jesus Christ on Calvary.

And it had made me his forever.

Now I understood why the world was so strange to me when I had not yet experienced this adventure or felt this fire.

But I also understood that everyone, and everything, would be saved.

It Is Easter

Death could no longer be far off, and now it was easy for me to repeat:

> *"Such the joy that I await,*
> *that every sorrow is my delight."*

The passage of the fire of the Spirit upon my flesh had made the reality of invisible things infinitely evident.

Everything was normal again now. Nature was once again the external sign of the things I had seen.

The course of the seasons, birth and dying, the rising of the sun and its setting—everything was the faithful recall of what the fire had shown me, which was the theme of everything real.

Life and death were but two aspects of one and the same thing, as also sorrow and joy, light and darkness, cold and heat.

It was as if the real were cut in half by a door.

It was with good reason that Christ had presented himself in this way: "I am the door."

The door is the same one on both sides.

The earth, the visible, the sensible, time, and space, are

on this side; heaven, the invisible, the eternal, the infinite, are on the other side.

But everything is one, logical, and true.

The door that is Christ is Lord at once of the here and the beyond, as Christ is crucified here and glorious beyond.

To become immortal, to enter into the glory of the Risen Christ, every person must pass through this door, and the One who opens and closes it is the Lord. As Revelation says, *"If I open, no one closes."*

This passage is called Easter, and the first to make it was Christ the Lord—as it is said, "This is the Pasch of the Lord."

Everything on this side of the door has its meaning, and can be understood, only in function of, in the embrace of, what is beyond.

Short of this relationship, the succession of things here below cannot involve the real, and you use up your life without seeing.

Things in time without any reference to the eternal acquire no meaning. They are as nothing, like dried-up leaves. Jesus himself said: *"Do not store up treasures for yourselves on earth, where moths and woodworms destroy them and thieves can break in and steal."*

And he added, *"But store up treasures for yourselves in heaven, where neither moth nor woodworms destroy and thieves cannot break in and steal"* (Matt. 6:19–20).

The resurrection of Christ gives meaning and life to every creature, as created by the Father, and actualized in view of, and through, Jesus Christ.

And creatures, through him, have two faces: one crucified, here, and one glorious, beyond.

No person can escape this reality, and this is why the death of each one of us has a sorrowful face in reality and a glorious face in hope.

The passage is always a terrible trial, like coming to a boundless sea—and then there is the explosion of joy as you watch the sea open.

So it was for the People of God, and so it is for us.

There is always the painful wait, and then a sudden light.

The wait is yours, the light is God's.

And it is gratuitous.

You can never claim you deserved it.

On the contrary!

No merit has the power to open the door.

It is only the gratuity of God's love that can manage this impassable lock.

"When he closes, nobody can open" (Rev. 3:7).

But his will is always prompt to open, for *"I have come that they may have life and have it to the full"* (John 10:10).

How often have you asked, "Why am I still here?"

And the reply is ever the same.

You must learn to love. For beyond the door there is nothing but love.

❧

When I realized that I had pierced hands and feet, and especially that I had a cleft in my side, I understood what it meant to love without trifling.

Love is indeed a serious thing, and terribly challenging.

When I thought of my past life, even as a child, at that moment I could only feel myself to have been poor and sinful.

"Poor" now meant poor in love.

"Sinful" meant, "You have trifled with someone who was suffering for you."

The weight of this vision of things is awful.

And yet these things are true, and we must not forget them too easily.

It is an ugly thing to step across the corpse of the one who died for you, and pass by singing when someone is suffering for you.

The law of love demands reparation. Instead, we forget all about it.

We should not be astonished if God sometimes makes us stand trembling at the gate.

☙

After Saint Michael's Fast of September, 1224, I felt my passage very near. Every least movement reminded me.

Since I could no longer walk I rode a donkey. And always before me was the back of Fra Leo, who had always been so devoted and so faithful and was the one person to whom I confided the sight of my wounds.

It was repugnant to me when others curiously sought me out. I felt as if I were divulging a secret meant only for me and for Fra Leo, who had been the one to gather me up in his arms at Sasso Spico like a wounded wretch.

Riding along on the donkey I saw my Umbria once more, and with what joy! The Marches too. And it was sweet to speak a word of comfort to those I met along the way.

Naturally I was a guest at Saint Damian, and I saw Clare. I stayed there a little while.

I felt so at home in the little hut of branches which they had built for me against the wall. And so at ease by the side of a woman so strong and so good, who had kept faithful to the poverty of the Gospel to the last.

When I looked at Clare all my problems disappeared. The everlasting complications of the brethren, whether it was possible or impossible to live poverty in real life, found their answer in the life of this creature.

Live, don't discuss, she seemed to say with her sweet person.

And there was another comfort for me in this period.

It was the answer to a prayer that I had been making for some time now. I knew the answer would come.

God is so tender towards us!

It was the matter of an ancient quarrel between the Bishop and the Mayor of Assisi.

How I had suffered on its account! For it was a scandal to so many. Besides, it seemed to me that Assisi ought always to be a city of peace.

Well, one morning I felt the need of going to the city, and Fra Leo saddled up the donkey.

The wounds were hurting terribly, but I felt I had to go.

What a hubbub around me as I neared Assisi!

I felt the love of my friends press around my sorrow.

What a grand thing, friendship!

How sweet, compassion!

Our route took us before the episcopal palace. I was motioned to enter, and the donkey passed the portal of the courtyard.

I could not help but be surprised! Before me, side by side, stood the Bishop and the Mayor. They were simply standing there, looking at me.

I understood. They had made peace. And they wanted to tell me:

It was a beautiful thing. People were weeping for joy.

Then I opened my mouth, and in chorus with my brothers, with what was left of my voice, I sang:

> *All praise be yours, my Lord,*
> *through those who grant pardon for love of you;*
> *those who endure*
> *sickness and trial.*
> *Happy those who endure in peace,*
> *by you, Most High, they will be crowned.*

But now the time had come for me to pass through the door.

I had never been afraid of Christ, and after the revelation at Saint Damian I felt him to be a friend close and true.

I even came to the point of being able to say, for it seemed to me to be quite true:

> *"Life to me, of course, is Christ,*
> *but then death would bring me something more"*
> (Phil. 1:21)

These words of Paul to the Philippians had always been a help to me. But now they gave me real courage.

Meanwhile however I felt weaker and weaker.

More and more doctors surrounded me. It was beginning to look like a siege.

Bishop Hugo wished to lodge me in his own house, so just on my account he went off on pilgrimage to Mount Gargano, a place renowned in those days for its shrine of Saint Michael.

But I felt that the door was opening now.

I loved to recite Psalm 142, especially because of the mighty words that were now my continual prayer: "Free me from this imprisonment" (Ps. 142:7).

Yes, this is the manner in which I would pray at the moment of my passage.

But for now I returned impetuously to my own psalm, my life's psalm, which I had composed myself, steeping my pen in the beauties of my earth: "The Canticle of the Creatures."

> *All praise be yours, my Lord, through Sister Death,*
> *From whose embrace no mortal can escape.*
> *Woe to those who die in mortal sin!*
> *Happy those she finds doing your will!*
> *The second death can do no harm to them.*
> *Praise and bless my Lord, and give him thanks,*
> *   and serve him with great humility*

When I felt the hour had come, I begged to be borne to the Portiuncula, my mother church, the place of my predilection, my Order's Bethlehem—my intuition and perception of God's mercy and pardon.

On our way through Assisi I asked to pause a moment at the lepers' hospital.

My litter was placed on the ground and I asked to be turned toward the city.

I wanted to bless it. I wept and I suffered, but I was happy.

> *"Blessed be thou by God, thou holy faithful city,*
> *for through thee many souls shall be saved,*
> *within thee many servants of God shall dwell,*
> *from thee shall many be chosen for the realms of life*
>   *eternal."*

And when I lowered my arm again to my pallet a most sweet thought came over me.

I could not see the city towers, but I felt them as I breathed.

I could not see Subasio, but I felt its color.

I thought.

The Lord most high has made an exception for me, Francis, and what an exception!

Scripture says, "A prophet is only despised in his own country" (Mark 6:4).

And it says this in order to recall the mystery of rejection, the rejection of those who have been most cruelly subject to it.

Jesus himself had known the suffering of his rejection by Nazareth, his "native land."

For me, Jesus had made an exception.

Assisi had not rejected me. On the contrary it had loved me. And I so loved this little city as well, so lovely, so tender, so hospitable.

Then I was carried to the Portiuncula. With what affection was I surrounded! For it was here that I desired to make my "Easter communion."

It was a Saturday. A good sign! The third of October.

I was almost entirely blind now; the life of my eyes was already at an end.

Around me I could hear my companions. How many there were! What rustling! What expectation!

It was like being part of a liturgical function, lively as if it had been taking place in a cathedral.

As if I had been Master of Ceremonies, I asked to be borne out of doors, into the open air, under the trees.

They bore me there.

All around, the creatures whom I could no longer see in my blindness spoke to me tenderly.

I would have said that they too prayed, along with my stricken friars.

When I perceived that the hour was at hand, I ordered them to lay me naked on the naked earth.

I say "ordered," for it was not easy to make them obey.

There are always those who think this passage something foreign, impossible, inappropriate, something always to be fled. But no, here it was, and I desired it.

The moist earth afforded some alleviation for my pain. It was like a familiar embrace, once again beginning to press me close.

But this embrace I sought no longer.

The true embrace, I now awaited from him—my Most High Lord.

I entered the gate. It seemed to me I heard a choir.

Perhaps it was the angels of that little Church of Saint Mary of the Angels. It had always been my favorite one.

PRAYING
WITH SAINT FRANCIS

A Little Divine Office,
Composed from His Words
and from His Prayers

I have tried to bring Francis of Assisi back to you. I hope I
have brought him very near.

It has not been difficult for me to feel him alive, to hear his
words as if they were being spoken now; for I am bound to
him, and to the universality of his message, by love.
   As I have already said, Francis is within each of us.

I was tempted to call this little volume *My Francis*, and this
would surely have been more precise. I think, however, that
each of you will be able to do this. You can call it *My Francis*.

I have certainly not been very discreet in calling it *I, Francis*.
   Pardon me, if you will—you also, my readers—for I hope I
have been pardoned by him, Francis: in any case, now that
my toil is at an end he invites me, person of high prayer that

he was, to say some of his prayers with him (as a penance or as a reward, who can say?).

I admit I have had to be just a bit inventive here. I have put his prayers together from here and there; but the prayers are his. And—inveterate monk that I am—I have arranged them in the form of monastic hours, a kind of Office composed by him, by Francis, that man of prayer.

To say that they are beautiful would be superfluous. These are prayers written by a saint.

The Psalms, of course, are from the Psalter of the Church, but the arrangement of their verses is his, and reflects his attitude of mind.

For each canonical hour I have set down a *Psalm*, a *Reading*, taken from his works, and a *Prayer*.

The hours can be prayed all on one day, or they can be spread over several days. What is important is to be at peace and read with calm.

Invitatory Hymn:
God's Praises

Letter to Fra Leo

You alone are holy, Lord God, Worker of Wonders.
You are mighty.
You are great.
You are the Most High.
You are omnipotent, our holy Father, King of heaven
    and earth.
You, Lord God, three and one, are our every good.
You, Lord God, all good, our highest good—Lord God
    living and true.
You are charity and love.
You are wisdom.
You are humility.
You are patience.
You are security.
You are peace.
You are joy and gladness.
You are justice and temperance.
You are riches altogether sufficient.

You are beauty.
You are meekness.
You are our protector.
You are our strength.
You are our refreshment.
You are our hope.
You are our faith.
You are our most profound sweetness.
You are our eternal life, great and admirable Lord,
    omnipotent God, merciful Savior!

Matins

Psalm

Shout for joy to honor God our strength, acclaim God
with shouts of joy (Ps. 81:2; 47:1).

For Yahweh, the Most High, is to be dreaded, the great
King of the whole world (Ps. 47:3).

For the Father who is in heaven, our King from the first,
has dispatched his beloved Son from on high, to be born
of the blessed Virgin Mary (Ps. 74:12; cf. John 3:13 and the
Nicene Creed).

"He will invoke me: 'You are my Father.' And I shall make
him my first-born, the Most High for kings on the earth" (Ps.
89:27–28).

In the daytime may Yahweh command his love to come,
and by night may his song be on my lips (Ps. 42:8). This is a
day made memorable by Yahweh, what immense joy for us!
(Ps. 118:24).

For the most holy infant whom we love has been given to
us, and is born for us, along the road, and placed in a man-
ger, for there was no room in the inn (Isa. 9:6, Luke 2:7).

Glory to God in the highest heavens; peace to men and
women who enjoy his favor (Luke 2:14).

Let the heavens be glad, let earth rejoice, let the sea thunder and all that it holds, let the fields exult and all that is in them, let all the woodland trees cry out for joy (Ps. 96:11–12).

Sing Yahweh a new song, sing to Yahweh, all the earth, sing to Yahweh, bless his Name (Ps. 96:1). Yahweh is great, loud must be his praise, he is to be feared beyond all gods (Ps. 96:4).

Pay tribute to Yahweh, families of the peoples, tribute to Yahweh of glory and power, tribute to Yahweh of his name's due glory (Ps. 96:7).

Offer him your lives, and bear his holy cross; fulfill to the limit his holy commands (Rom. 12:1, Luke 14:27).

Reading

The Praise of Virtue

I salute you, Queen Wisdom. May the Lord safeguard you with your holy sister, pure and holy simplicity.

Holy Lady Poverty! May the Lord watch over you and your sister, holy humility.

Holy Lady Charity! May the Lord watch over you and your sister, holy obedience.

May the Lord protect your holy virtues, one and all, for you find your source in him and come forth from him.

No one in this world can possess you without dying to self.

Those who possess one of you, without offending the others, possess all.

Those who offend one of you lack all and offend against all.

Each of you drives out vice and sin.

Holy Wisdom overcomes Satan and his wiles.

Holy and pure simplicity confounds the wisdom of this world and fleshly desires.

Holy poverty drives out cupidity, avarice, and earthly desires.

Holy humility overcomes pride, the people of this world, and all terrestrial things.

Holy charity confounds all temptations of the flesh and the devil and all human fears.

Holy obedience confounds all carnal and bodily desires and keeps the body in check. It holds us subject to the Spirit and obedient to our brothers and sisters. It keeps us submissive to all the men and women of the world, and not only to human beings, but to the animals and beasts, who can do what they want with us to the extent that God has given them power over us.

Prayer

> Almighty, eternal,
> just, and merciful God,
> grant to us wretches, by your will,
> to do what we know you wish,
> and ever to wish what pleases you:
> in order that, purified in soul,
> lighted up within
> and inflamed by the fire of the Holy Spirit,
> we may follow the footsteps of your Son,
> our Lord Jesus Christ,
> and to reach you, Most High,
> by your grace alone.
> For you live and reign and are glorified,
> in perfect Trinity
> and simple Unity,
> Almighty God,
> for ever and ever. Amen.
> *Letter of Saint Francis to the Chapter of Friars*

Lauds

Psalm

The Canticle of Creatures

Most high, all-powerful, all good, Lord!
   All praise is yours, all glory, all honour
   And all blessing.
To you alone, Most High, do they belong.
   No mortal lips are worthy
   To pronounce your name.
All praise be yours, my Lord, through all that you have
made,
   And first my lord Brother Sun,
   Who brings the day; and light you give to us through him.
How beautiful is he, how radiant in all his splendour!
   Of you, Most High, he bears the likeness.
All praise be yours, my Lord, through Sister Moon and Stars;
   In the heavens you have made them, bright
   And precious and fair.
All praise be yours, my Lord, through Brothers Wind and
air,

And fair and stormy, all the weather's moods,
By which you cherish all that you have made.
All praise be yours, my Lord, through Sister Water,
So useful, lowly, precious and pure.
All praise be yours, my Lord, through Brother Fire,
Through whom you brighten up the night.
How beautiful is he, how gay! Full of power and strength.
All praise be yours, my Lord, through Sister Earth, our
mother,
Who feeds us in her sovereignty and produces
Various fruits with coloured flowers and herbs.
All praise be yours, my Lord, through those who grant pardon
For love of you; through those who endure
Sickness and trial.
Happy those who endure in peace,
By you, Most High, they will be crowned.
All praise be yours, my Lord, through Sister Death,
From whose embrace no mortal can escape.
Woe to those who die in mortal sin!
Happy those She finds doing your will!
The second death can do no harm to them.
Praise and bless my Lord, and give him thanks,
And serve him with great humility.[*]

Reading

From the Testament

Thus did the Lord grant to me, Fra Francis, to begin to
do penance: when I was in my sins it was too bitter to me to

---

[*] *St. Francis of Assisi: Writings and Early Biographies*, an English Omnibus of
Sources for the Life of St. Francis, ed. Marion A. Habig (Chicago: Franciscan
Herald Press, 1973), pp. 130–131.

look upon lepers; and the same Lord led me through them, and by them I experienced mercy.

And as I went among them, what had seemed to me bitter before, was changed for me into sweetness of spirit and of body.

Prayer

Prayer Before a Crucifix

> O high and glorious God,
> enlighten my heart.
> Give me unwavering faith,
> sure hope,
> and perfect love.
> Give me deep humility,
> wisdom, and knowledge,
> that I may keep your commandments. Amen.

Prime

Psalm

In you, Yahweh, I take shelter, never let me be disgraced.
In your righteousness rescue me, deliver me, turn your ear to
me and save me (Ps. 71:1-2).

Be a sheltering rock for me, a walled fortress to save me.
For you alone are my hope. Lord, Yahweh, I have trusted you
since my youth (Ps. 71:3-5).

You have been my portion from my mother's womb and
the constant theme of my praise (Ps. 71:6).

My mouth is full of your praises: full of your splendor all
day long (Ps. 71:8).

In your loving kindness, answer me, Yahweh, in your
tenderness turn to me (Ps. 69:16).

Do not hide your face from your servant, quick, I am in
trouble, answer me (Ps. 69:17).

Blessed be Yahweh, my rock . . . my citadel, my savior (Ps.
114:1-2).

My Strength, I play for you, my citadel is God himself, the
God who loves me (Ps. 59:17).

Reading

And those who came to embrace this life gave to the poor everything they might have, and were content with a simple tunic, bound if they wished with a cord before and behind, and underclothing. And they did not wish to have more.

We clerics said the Office with the rest of the clergy. And we were very willing to be in the church, and were simple and subject to all. And I labored with my hands, and wished to labor; and I firmly wish all the other friars to labor, in honest toil, and not from cupidity of money, but for the sake of example and to ward off idleness.

Prayer

My Lord Jesus Christ,
I thank you
for such great love and charity
which you show in my regard.
I have learned that it is a sign of great love
when the Lord punishes his servant,
for all his or her defects in this world,
in order not to punish him or her in the next.
And I am prepared and ready
joyfully to undergo every trial
and every adversity which you, O God,
wish to send me
for my sins.

Third Consideration upon the Sacred Stigmata

Terce

Psalm

Clap your hands, all you peoples, acclaim God with shouts of joy, for Yahweh, the Most High, is to be dreaded, the great King of the whole world (Ps. 47:1-2).

God, my king from the first, author of saving acts throughout the earth (Ps. 74:12).

Let the heavens be glad, let the earth rejoice, let the sea thunder and all that it holds, let the fields exult and all that is in them, let the woodland trees cry out for joy (Ps. 96:11-12).

Sing Yahweh a new song! Sing to Yahweh, all the earth! Sing to Yahweh, bless his name. Proclaim his salvation day after day, tell his glory among the nations, tell his marvels to every people. Yahweh is great, loud must be his praise, he is to be feared beyond all gods (Ps. 96:1-4).

Pay tribute to Yahweh, families of the peoples, tribute to Yahweh of glory and power, tribute to Yahweh of his name's due glory (Ps. 96:7-8).

Offer him your lives, and bear his holy cross: fulfill to the limit his holy commands (cf. Luke 14:27).

Tremble before him, all the earth! Say among the nations, "Yahweh is king!" (Ps. 96:9-10).

And he rose higher than all the heavens, and sits at the right hand of God, the Father most holy! (Eph. 4:10; Nicene Creed).

Cry out for joy at the presence of Yahweh, for he comes, he comes to judge the earth, to judge the world with justice and the nations with his truth (Ps. 96:13).

Reading

From the Testament

Then the Lord gave me, and he still gives me, great faith in priests who live according to the form of the Holy Roman Church, because of their sacred orders, and if I were to be persecuted, I would fly to them for refuge. And if I had wisdom to shame Solomon, and I found poor and humble secular priests, I would not wish to preach in the parishes in which they were assigned without their leave.

And I will fear and love them and all their brothers, and honor them as my lords.

Prayer

> May the burning and tender might
> of your love,
> I beseech you, O Lord,
> ravish my soul,
> and carry it far from all that is of this earth,
> that I may die
> for love of your love,
> as you deigned to die
> for love of my love.
> *Ubertino da Casale*, Arbor Vitae Crucifixae Jesu,
> *Book V, Chapter 4*

Sext

Psalm

May Yahweh answer you in time of trouble, may the name of the God of Jacob protect you! May he send you help from the sanctuary, give you support from Zion, remember all your oblations and find your holocaust acceptable; may he grant you your heart's desire, and crown all your plans with success (Ps. 20:1-4).

May we shout with joy for your victory . . . we boast about the name of Yahweh, our God (Ps. 20:5-7).

May Yahweh grant all your petitions; now I know that the Lord has sent us his Son, Jesus Christ, and that he will judge the world according to justice (Ps. 20:5, 9:8; cf. John 4:9).

May Yahweh be a stronghold for the oppressed, a stronghold when times are hard. Those who acknowledge your name can rely on you, you never desert those who seek you, Yahweh (Ps. 9:9-10).

You have always been my citadel, a shelter when I am in trouble (Ps. 59:16).

My citadel is God himself, the God who loves me (Ps. 59:17).

Reading

To the Rulers of Peoples

To all magistrates and consuls, to all judges and governors all over the world and to everyone else who receives this letter, Brother Francis, your poor worthless servant in the Lord God, sends greetings and peace.

Consider and realize that the day of death is approaching. I therefore beg of you with all the respect I am capable of that you do not forget God or swerve from his commandments because of the worldly cares and anxieties which you have to shoulder. For all who forget him and *turn away from his commandments* (Ps. 118:21) *shall be forgotten* by him (Ezek. 33:13). When the day of death comes, all that they thought their own will be taken away from them. The more wisdom and power they enjoyed in this life, the greater the torments they will have to endure in hell.

And so, my lords, this is my advice. Put away all worry and anxiety and receive the holy Body and Blood of our Lord Jesus Christ fervently in memory of him. See to it that God is held in great reverence among your subjects; every evening, at a signal given by a herald or in some other way, praise and thanks should be given to the Lord God almighty by all the people. If you refuse to see to this, you can be sure that you will be held to account for it at the day of judgment before Jesus Christ, your Lord and God.

Those who keep a copy of this letter and put its prescriptions into practice can rest assured that they have God's blessing.[*]

---

[*]Omnibus of Sources, pp. 115–116.

Prayer

> Lord God,
> Father of glory,
> we pray:
> By your mercy,
> show us
> what we should do!
> *Anonymous Perugianus, 10*

Nones

Psalm

Take pity on me, God, take pity on me, in you my soul takes shelter (Ps. 57:1).

Full of hope, I take shelter in the shadow of your wings, until the destroying storm is over (Ps. 57:1).

I call on God Most High, on God who has done everything for me (Ps. 57:2).

To send from heaven and save me, to check the people harrying me (Ps. 57:3).

May God send his faithfulness and love. He sends from on high and takes me, he draws me from deep waters, he delivers me from my powerful enemy, from a foe too strong for me.

They laid a net where I was walking when I was bowed with care; they dug a pitfall for me, but fell into it themselves (Ps. 57:3, 18:16, 57:6).

My heart is ready, God, my heart is ready; I mean to sing and play for you (Ps. 57:7).

Awake, muse, awake, lyre and harp, I mean to wake the dawn! (Ps. 57:8).

Lord, I mean to thank you among the peoples . . . your

love is high as heaven, your faithfulness as the clouds (Ps.
57:9–10).

Rise high above the heavens, God, let your glory be over
the earth (Ps. 57:11).

Reading

From the Little Flowers

Fra Francis and Fra Masseo arrived in a little village rather
hungry, and, according to the Rule, they went begging their
bread for love of God; and Saint Francis went by one road
and Fra Masseo by another. But in as much as Saint Francis
was a person of altogether humble mien and small stature,
he was accounted a lowly pauper by those who did not know
him, and received nothing but a few blows along with some
crusts of dry bread; but Fra Masseo, being a tall person and
handsome, was given good bread, sometimes even whole
loaves.

Having gathered what they could, they met to eat at a
certain spot outside the village where there was a beautiful
spring, with a large, beautiful rock, upon which each placed
all the alms he had received. And Saint Francis, seeing that
Fra Masseo's pieces of bread were more numerous, more
beautiful, and larger than his own, rejoiced greatly, and
spoke thus: "O Fra Masseo, we are not worthy of such a
great treasure!" And he repeated these words several times,
until Fra Masseo asked, "Father, how can these be called
treasure, when they are consumed in such poverty and lack
of necessities? Here is neither knife, nor fork, nor porringer,
nor roof, nor table, nor steward, nor maid!" Saint Francis
replied, "And this is what I esteem as treasure—where there
is no single appurtenance provided by human industry, but
where all has been procured by divine providence alone, as is
evident in the bread we have received, in the rock table that

is so beautiful, and in this spring so clear. And I do hope
that this treasure of noble, holy poverty, served to us by God
himself, may make us love with all our heart." And with
these words said, and prayer having been made, and corporal
refreshment having been taken of those pieces of bread and
that water, they rose and set out for France.

Prayer

> May the burning and tender might
> of your love,
> I beseech you, O Lord,
> ravish my soul,
> and carry it far from all that is of this earth,
> that I may die
> for love of your love,
> as you deigned to die
> for love of my love.

Vespers

Psalm

Sing Yahweh a new song, for he has performed marvels, his own right hand, his holy arm gives him the power to save the one whom the Father consecrated (Ps. 98:1; cf. John 10:36).

Yahweh has displayed his power; has revealed his righteousness to the nations (Ps. 98:2).

In the daytime may Yahweh command his love to come, and by night may his song be on my lips (Ps. 42:8).

This is the day made memorable by Yahweh, what immense joy for us! (Ps. 118:24).

Blessings on him who comes in the name of Yahweh . . . Yahweh is God, he smiles on us (Ps. 118:27).

Let the heavens be glad, let the earth rejoice, let the sea thunder and all that it holds, let the fields exult and all that is in them, let the woodland trees cry out for joy (Ps. 96:11–12).

Pay tribute to Yahweh, families of the people, tribute to Yahweh of glory and power, tribute to Yahweh of his name's due glory (Ps. 96:7–8).

O kingdoms of the earth, sing to God; sing to the Lord,

who mounts above the heaven of heavens in the east.

Behold, he will make heard the might of his voice: give glory to God for Israel: his power and his might are among the clouds.

Reading

Concerning True and Perfect Gladness

One day, in the vicinity of Saint Mary of the Angels, Blessed Francis called Fra Leone and said to him, "Fra Leone, write." The latter responded, "Behold, I am ready." "Write," said the other, "what true gladness is."

"A messenger comes, and says that all the masters of Paris have entered the Order. Write, 'This is not true gladness.' Or again, all the prelates of Europe, archbishops and bishops, have entered the Order—and the Kings of France and England to boot. Write, 'This is not true gladness.' And if you should receive word besides that my friars have gone among the infidels and converted them all to the faith, or that I have received from God the grace to heal the sick and to work many miracles—well, I tell you, not even this is true gladness."

"But what is true gladness?"

"Suppose that returning from Perugia in the middle of the night, I arrive here. And the winter is most muddy, and so cold that the icicles which have formed upon the hem of my tunic are beating against my legs continually, so that blood is flowing from the wounds they have made. And I, all in mud and cold and ice, arrive at the door. Long do I knock and cry, and a friar comes and asks, 'Who is it?' And I reply, 'Fra Francis.' And he says, 'Go away, this is no decent hour of the night to arrive. You shall not enter.' I insist; but the other replies, 'Go away, you are a simpleton and an idiot. You cannot come in here anymore. We are not in need of the likes of you.' And still I remain before the door, and say, 'For the love of God, receive me for this night!' And he responds, 'I shall not. Go ask the Crucifers.'

"Now, if I shall have had patience, and shall not have become disturbed and angry, I tell you this is true gladness, and this is true virtue and the soul's salvation."

Prayer

> We adore you,
> Lord Jesus Christ,
> here, and in all your churches
> throughout the world,
> and we bless you,
> for by your holy cross
> you have redeemed the world.
> *Testament of Saint Francis*

Compline

Who are you, Lord of infinite goodness,
and wisdom and power,
that you deign to visit me
who am vile vermin
and one abominable?

Psalm

I give thanks to you, Yahweh, Father most holy, King of
sky and earth, for you have given me consolation (Isa. 12:1;
cf. Matt. 11:25).

See now, he is the God of my salvation. I have trust now
and no fear (Isa. 12:2).

Yahweh is my strength and my song, he has been my
savior (Ps. 118:14).

Your right hand, Yahweh, shows majestic in power, your
right hand, Yahweh, shatters the enemy. So great your splendor you crush your foes (Exod. 15:6–7).

Yahweh will always hear those who are in need . . . Let
heaven and earth acclaim him, the oceans and all that move
in them!

For God will save Zion, and rebuild the towns of Judah:

they will be lived in, owned, handed down to his servants' descendants and lived in by those who love his name (Ps. 69:33–36).

Reading

From the Testament

And the Lord gave me such faith in the Church, that I simply adored him and prayed thus: "We adore you, Lord Jesus Christ, who are in all the churches of the whole world, and we bless you, for by means of your holy cross you have redeemed the world."

Prayer

> My Lord Jesus Christ,
> two graces I beg you to grant me
> before I die:
> the first is that in my lifetime
> I may feel, in my soul and in my body,
> as far as possible,
> that sorrow which you, tender Jesus,
> underwent in the hour
> of your most bitter passion;
> the second is that I may feel in my heart,
> as far as possible,
> that abundance of love with which you,
> son of God,
> were inflamed, so as willingly to undergo
> such a great passion for us sinners.
> *Third Consideration upon the Sacred Stigmata*

With Mary

Greeting to the Blessed Virgin

> Hail, holy Lady,
>> Most holy Queen,
>> Mary, Mother of God,
>> Ever Virgin;
> Chosen by the most holy Father in heaven,
>> Consecrated by him,
>> With his most holy beloved Son
>> And the Holy Spirit, the Comforter.
> On you descended and in you still remains
>> All the fullness of grace
>> And every good.
> Hail, his Palace.
> Hail, his Tabernacle.
> Hail, his Robe.
> Hail, his Handmaid.
> Hail, his Mother.
> And Hail, all holy Virtues,
>> Who, by the grace
>> And inspiration of the Holy Spirit,

Are poured into the hearts of the faithful
So that, faithless no longer,
They may be made faithful servants of God
Through you.[*]

---

[*]Omnibus of Sources, pp. 135–136.